MW00772330

The Book of Occasional Services • 2003

Conforming to General Convention 2003

CHURCH PUBLISHING
New York

Church Publishing
19 E. 34th St.
New York, NY 10016

6 5 4 3 2

Table of Contents

Pastoral Services

Episcopal Services

Preface

The Book of Occasional Services is a collection of liturgical resources related to occasions which do not occur with sufficient frequency to warrant their inclusion in The Book of Common Prayer. As provided for in the copyright statement, it is expected that the materials to be used for a specific occasion will be reproduced locally for that use.

All of the material in this book is optional. None of it is required, and no congregation is likely to make use of all of it.

The materials included in this collection come from a variety of sources. Generally, they arise out of the specific use of worshipping communities engaged in the process of creating liturgical responses to particular occasions in the life of the church. A previous edition, for example, included for the first time liturgical forms to accompany the preparation of adults for baptism.

It is intended that the collection will evolve as the church continues to discover opportunities to address the life of the Christian community in liturgy. As the church expresses the need for additional occasional liturgical materials, and as the General Convention authorizes the use of those materials, new editions of this book will be prepared and published. (Each successive printing of the book will bear in the title, the date of the General Convention to which it responds.)

Every worshipping community in the church has an important role to play in the ongoing development of this worship resource. The Standing Liturgical Commission is anxious to hear about the use of the liturgies in this volume, and welcomes suggestions and examples of additional liturgical forms to include in future editions.

The Church Year

Anthems at the Candle Lighting

The anthems (Lucernaria) which follow are intended for optional use at the Order of Worship for the Evening as provided for in the second rubric on page 112 of the Prayer Book. They are arranged for responsorial performance by a cantor or reader and the congregation. All repeat the complete refrain after the cantor, and the second half of the refrain after the verse which follows. The Lucernarium then concludes with the first half of the Gloria Patri, followed by the complete refrain.

The Versicle which follows is sung or said by the officiant or by a cantor. Any of the Versicles may be used with any of the Lucernaria.

When these anthems are used, it is appropriate to omit the Short Lesson which precedes the Prayer for Light.

1

You, O Lord, are my lamp; *
my God, you make my darkness bright.
You, O Lord, are my lamp;
my God, you make my darkness bright.
You have been my helper:
My God, you make my darkness bright.
Glory to the Father, and to the Son, and to the Holy Spirit.
You, O Lord, are my lamp;
my God, you make my darkness bright.

V. Let my prayer be set forth, O Lord:
R. As incense in your sight.

2

The Lord is my light * and my salvation.
The Lord is my light and my salvation.
The Lord is the strength of my life:
And my salvation.
Glory to the Father, and to the Son, and to the Holy Spirit.
The Lord is my light and my salvation.

V. I will bless the Lord at all times:
R. His praise shall ever be in my mouth.

3

With you, O Lord, is the well of life, *
and in your light we see light.
With you, O Lord, is the well of life,
and in your light we see light.
Your love, O Lord, reaches to the heavens,
and your faithfulness to the clouds:
And in your light we see light.
Glory to the Father, and to the Son, and to the Holy Spirit.
With you, O Lord, is the well of life,
and in your light we see light.

V. Abide with us, O Lord:
R. For it is toward evening.

4

From the rising of the sun to its going down, *
let the Name of the Lord be praised.
From the rising of the sun to its going down,
let the Name of the Lord be praised.
From this time forth for evermore:

Let the Name of the Lord be praised.
Glory to the Father, and to the Son, and to the Holy Spirit.
From the rising of the sun to its going down,
let the Name of the Lord be praised.

V. The sun knows the time of its setting:
R. You make darkness that it may be night.

The anthems which follow may be used at the times indicated.
Alternatively, one of the general Lucernaria given above may be used,
followed by the appropriate seasonal Versicle.

Advent

Come and save us, * O Lord God of hosts.
Come and save us, O Lord God of hosts.
Show the light of your countenance, and we shall be saved:
O Lord God of hosts.
Glory to the Father, and to the Son, and to the Holy Spirit.
Come and save us, O Lord God of hosts.

V. Show us your mercy, O Lord:
R. And grant us your salvation.

Christmas

The Word was made flesh, * alleluia, alleluia.
The Word was made flesh, alleluia, alleluia.
And dwelt among us:
Alleluia, alleluia.
Glory to the Father, and to the Son, and to the Holy Spirit.
The Word was made flesh, alleluia, alleluia.

V. Blessed is he who comes in the name of the Lord, alleluia:
R. God is the Lord; he has shined upon us, alleluia.

Epiphany   *(through the following Saturday evening)*

All nations shall be blessed in him, *   and do him service.
All nations shall be blessed in him, and do him service.
All kings shall bow down before him:
And do him service.
Glory to the Father, and to the Son, and to the Holy Spirit.
All nations shall be blessed in him, and do him service.

V.   The kings of Tarshish and the isles shall pay tribute:
R.   The kings of Arabia and Saba shall offer gifts.

Lent

I make my prayer to you, O God; *   be merciful to me.
I make my prayer to you, O God; be merciful to me.
Heal my soul, for I have sinned against you:
Be merciful to me.
Glory to the Father, and to the Son, and to the Holy Spirit.
I make my prayer to you, O God, be merciful to me.

V.   Create in me a clean heart, O God:
R.   And renew a right spirit within me.

Easter   *(until Ascension Day)*

The Lord is risen from the tomb, *   alleluia, alleluia.
The Lord is risen from the tomb, alleluia, alleluia.
Who for our sake hung upon the Tree:
Alleluia, alleluia.
Glory to the Father, and to the Son, and to the Holy Spirit.
The Lord is risen from the tomb, alleluia, alleluia.

V.   The disciples were glad, alleluia:
R.   When they saw the risen Lord, alleluia.

Ascension *(until the Day of Pentecost)*

God has gone up with a shout, * alleluia, alleluia.
God has gone up with a shout, alleluia, alleluia.
The Lord with the sound of the ram's-horn:
Alleluia, alleluia.
Glory to the Father, and to the Son, and to the Holy Spirit.
God has gone up with a shout, alleluia, alleluia.

V. When Christ ascended up on high, alleluia:
R. He led captivity captive, alleluia.

The Day of Pentecost

The Spirit of the Lord now fills the whole world, *
alleluia, alleluia.
The Spirit of the Lord now fills the whole world,
alleluia, alleluia.
The Spirit who searches even the depths of God:
Alleluia, alleluia.
Glory to the Father, and to the Son, and to the Holy Spirit.
The Spirit of the Lord now fills the whole world,
alleluia, alleluia.

V. The apostles spoke in other tongues, alleluia:
R. The wonderful works of God, alleluia.

Trinity Sunday

Glory to you, O Lord, * in the high vault of heaven.
Glory to you, O Lord, in the high vault of heaven.
You are worthy of glory and praise for ever:
In the high vault of heaven.
Glory to the Father, and to the Son, and to the Holy Spirit.
Glory to you, O Lord, in the high vault of heaven.

V. Let us glorify the Lord: Father, Son, and Holy Spirit:
R. Praise him and highly exalt him for ever.

Feasts of the Incarnation

The Word was made flesh, * and dwelt among us.
The Word was made flesh, and dwelt among us.
He was with God in the beginning:
And dwelt among us.
Glory to the Father, and to the Son, and to the Holy Spirit.
The Word was made flesh, and dwelt among us.

V. Blessed is he who comes in the name of the Lord:
R. God is the Lord; he has shined upon us.

*On Feasts of the Incarnation in Easter Season, the anthem and versicle
for Christmas Season are used.*

All Saints' Day and other Major Saints' Days

Let the righteous rejoice * in the presence of God.
Let the righteous rejoice in the presence of God.
Let them be merry and joyful:
In the presence of God.
Glory to the Father, and to the Son, and to the Holy Spirit.
Let the righteous rejoice in the presence of God.

V. Their sound has gone out into all lands:
R. And their message to the ends of the world.

Major Saints' Days in Easter Season

Their sound has gone out into all lands, * alleluia, alleluia.
Their sound has gone out into all lands, alleluia, alleluia.
And their message to the ends of the world:
Alleluia, alleluia.

Glory to the Father, and to the Son, and to the Holy Spirit.
Their sound has gone out into all lands, alleluia, alleluia.

V. Let the righteous rejoice, alleluia:
R. In the presence of God, alleluia.

Transfiguration and Holy Cross Day

When I am lifted up, * I will draw the whole world to myself.
When I am lifted up, I will draw the whole world to myself.
I am the light of the world:
I will draw the whole world to myself.
Glory to the Father, and to the Son, and to the Holy Spirit.
When I am lifted up, I will draw the whole world to myself.

V. All the ends of the earth shall see:
R. The salvation of our God.

*If, instead of one of the preceding anthems, it is desired to sing a
complete psalm at this point in the service, one of the evening psalms
listed on page 143 of the Prayer Book may be used.*

Anthems at the Breaking of Bread

One or more anthems may be used at the Breaking of the Bread.

The anthems (Confractoria) which follow are of varying length, and should be chosen on the basis of the time required for the Bread-breaking (whether of a whole loaf or of a number of large wafers), and for their seasonal appropriateness.

It should be noted that the rubrics of the Prayer Book require that the initial breaking of the Bread take place in silence. A distinct period of silence then follows (the celebrant having replaced the Bread on the paten). The singing of the Confractorium is then begun, during which the celebrant and other priests break the Bread for distribution. In the absence of a sufficient number of priests, deacons may assist in the Bread-breaking. The pouring of consecrated Wine into any additional chalices should also take place during this anthem, and before the Invitation "The Gifts of God . . . "and the celebrant's communion.

1

Christ our Passover is sacrificed for us;
Therefore let us keep the feast.

2

The bread which we break is a sharing in the Body of Christ.
We being many are one bread, one body,
for we all share in the one bread.

3

O Lamb of God, that takest away the sins of the world,
have mercy upon us.
O Lamb of God, that takest away the sins of the world,
have mercy upon us.
O Lamb of God, that takest away the sins of the world,
grant us thy peace.

4

Lamb of God, you take away the sins of the world:
have mercy on us.
Lamb of God, you take away the sins of the world:
have mercy on us.
Lamb of God, you take away the sins of the world:
grant us peace.

5

My flesh is food indeed, and my blood is drink indeed,
says the Lord.
My flesh is food indeed, and my blood is drink indeed,
says the Lord.
Those who eat my flesh and drink my blood dwell in me
and I in them.
My flesh is food indeed, and my blood is drink indeed,
says the Lord.

6

Whoever eats this bread will live for ever.
Whoever eats this bread will live for ever.
This is the true bread which comes down from heaven
and gives life to the world.
Whoever eats this bread will live for ever.

Whoever believes in me shall not hunger or thirst,
for the bread which I give for the life of the world
is my flesh.
Whoever eats this bread will live for ever.

Anthems 7 through 10 are not used in the season of Lent.

7

Alleluia. Christ our Passover is sacrificed for us;
Therefore let us keep the feast. Alleluia.

8

Alleluia.
Alleluia.
Christ our Passover is sacrificed for us;
therefore let us keep the feast.
Alleluia.

9

The disciples knew the Lord Jesus
in the breaking of the bread.
The disciples knew the Lord Jesus
in the breaking of the bread.
The bread which we break, alleluia,
is the communion of the body of Christ.
The disciples knew the Lord Jesus
in the breaking of the bread.
One body are we, alleluia,
for though many we share one bread.
The disciples knew the Lord Jesus
in the breaking of the bread.

10

Be known to us, Lord Jesus, in the breaking of the bread.
Be known to us, Lord Jesus, in the breaking of the bread.
The bread which we break, alleluia,
is the communion of the body of Christ.
Be known to us, Lord Jesus, in the breaking of the bread.
One body are we, alleluia,
for though many we share one bread.
Be known to us, Lord Jesus, in the breaking of the bread.

The following anthems may be used as separate pieces, or as refrains with selected verses from the psalms. In Easter Season, it is appropriate to add Alleluia (Hallelujah) to the anthem or refrain.

11

Blessed are those who are called to the Supper of the Lamb.

12

Whoever comes to me shall not hunger, and whoever believes in me shall never thirst.

13

Those who eat my flesh and drink my blood abide in me and I in them.

14

You shall eat and drink at my table in my kingdom, says the Lord.

15

Christ our Passover is sacrificed for us; therefore let us keep the feast.

Suggested Psalm Verses

Advent   Psalm 85:8-11

Christmas - 1 Epiphany   Psalm 96:8-11
                             Psalm 110:1-4

Lent   Psalm 106:4-5
           Psalm 108:3-6

Easter   Psalm 107:1-3,8
             Psalm 116:10-11,16-17

General   Psalm 34:3 & 8
              Psalm 43:3-4
              Psalm 103:1-4
              Psalm 105:1-4
              Psalm 117

Seasonal Blessings

The following blessings may be used by a bishop or priest whenever a blessing is appropriate.

Two forms of blessing are provided for each major season (except for Lent). The first is a three-fold form, with an Amen at the end of each sentence, leading into a trinitarian blessing. The second is a single-sentence formula leading directly into the blessing.

The formula for chanting these blessings is given in the musical appendix to the Altar Edition.

Advent Blessing

May Almighty God, by whose providence our Savior Christ came among us in great humility, sanctify you with the light of his blessing and set you free from all sin. *Amen.*

May he whose second Coming in power and great glory we await, make you steadfast in faith, joyful in hope, and constant in love. *Amen.*

May you, who rejoice in the first Advent of our Redeemer, at his second Advent be rewarded with unending life. *Amen.*

And the blessing of God Almighty, the Father, the Son, and the Holy Spirit, be upon you and remain with you for ever. *Amen.*

or this

May the Sun of Righteousness shine upon you and scatter the darkness from before your path; and the blessing of God Almighty, the Father, the Son, and the Holy Spirit, be among you, and remain with you always. *Amen.*

Christmas Season Blessing

May Almighty God, who sent his Son to take our nature upon him, bless you in this holy season, scatter the darkness of sin, and brighten your heart with the light of his holiness. *Amen.*

May God, who sent his angels to proclaim the glad news of the Savior's birth, fill you with joy, and make you heralds of the Gospel. *Amen.*

May God, who in the Word made flesh joined heaven to earth and earth to heaven, give you his peace and favor. *Amen.*

And the blessing of God Almighty, the Father, the Son, and the Holy Spirit, be upon you and remain with you for ever. *Amen.*

or this

May Christ, who by his Incarnation gathered into one things earthly and heavenly, fill you with his joy and peace; and the blessing of God Almighty, the Father, the Son, and the Holy Spirit, be among you, and remain with you always. *Amen.*

Epiphany

For use from the feast of the Epiphany through the following Sunday; and on the Second Sunday after the Epiphany in Year C.

May Almighty God, who led the Wise Men by the shining of a star to find the Christ, the Light from Light, lead you also, in your pilgrimage, to find the Lord. *Amen.*

May God, who sent the Holy Spirit to rest upon the Only-begotten at his baptism in the Jordan River, pour out that Spirit on you who have come to the waters of new birth. *Amen.*

May God, by the power that turned water into wine at the wedding feast at Cana, transform your lives and make glad your hearts. *Amen.*

And the blessing of God Almighty, the Father, the Son, and the Holy Spirit, be upon you and remain with you for ever. *Amen.*

or this

May Christ, the Son of God, be manifest in you, that your lives may be a light to the world; and the blessing of God Almighty, the Father, the Son, and the Holy Spirit, be among you, and remain with you always. *Amen.*

Lent

In Lent, in place of a seasonal blessing, a solemn Prayer over the People is used, as follows:

The Deacon or, in the absence of a deacon, the Celebrant says

Bow down before the Lord.

The people kneel and the Celebrant says one of the following prayers:

Ash Wednesday

Grant, most merciful Lord, to your faithful people pardon and peace, that they may be cleansed from all their sins, and serve you with a quiet mind; through Christ our Lord. *Amen.*

Lent 1

Grant, Almighty God, that your people may recognize their weakness and put their whole trust in your strength, so that they may rejoice for ever in the protection of your loving providence; through Christ our Lord. *Amen.*

Lent 2

Keep this your family, Lord, with your never-failing mercy, that relying solely on the help of your heavenly grace, they may be upheld by your divine protection; through Christ our Lord. *Amen.*

Lent 3

Look mercifully on this your family, Almighty God, that by your great goodness they may be governed and preserved evermore; through Christ our Lord. *Amen.*

Lent 4

Look down in mercy, Lord, on your people who kneel before you; and grant that those whom you have nourished by your Word and Sacraments may bring forth fruit worthy of repentance; through Christ our Lord. *Amen.*

Lent 5

Look with compassion, O Lord, upon this your people; that, rightly observing this holy season, they may learn to know you more fully, and to serve you with a more perfect will; through Christ our Lord. *Amen.*

From Palm Sunday through Maundy Thursday

Almighty God, we pray you graciously to behold this your family, for whom our Lord Jesus Christ was willing to be betrayed, and given into the hands of sinners, and to suffer death upon the cross; who lives and reigns for ever and ever. *Amen.*

Easter Season

May Almighty God, who has redeemed us and made us his children through the resurrection of his Son our Lord, bestow upon you the riches of his blessing. *Amen.*

May God, who through the water of baptism has raised us from sin into newness of life, make you holy and worthy to be united with Christ for ever. *Amen.*

May God, who has brought us out of bondage to sin into true and lasting freedom in the Redeemer, bring you to your eternal inheritance. *Amen.*

And the blessing of God Almighty, the Father, the Son, and the Holy Spirit, be upon you and remain with you for ever. *Amen.*

or this

The God of peace, who brought again from the dead our
Lord Jesus Christ, the great Shepherd of the sheep, through
the blood of the everlasting covenant, make you perfect in
every good work to do his will, working in you that which is
well-pleasing in his sight; and the blessing of God Almighty,
the Father, the Son, and the Holy Spirit, be among you, and
remain with you always. *Amen.*

The Day of Pentecost

May Almighty God, who enlightened the minds of the
disciples by pouring out upon them the Holy Spirit, make
you rich with his blessing, that you may abound more and
more in that Spirit for ever. *Amen.*

May God, who sent the Holy Spirit as a flame of fire that
rested upon the heads of the disciples, burn out all evil from
your hearts, and make them shine with the pure light of his
presence. *Amen.*

May God, who by the Holy Spirit caused those of many
tongues to proclaim Jesus as Lord, strengthen your faith and
send you out to bear witness to him in word and deed.
Amen.

And the blessing of God Almighty, the Father, the Son, and
the Holy Spirit, be upon you and remain with you for ever.
Amen.

or this

May the Spirit of truth lead you into all truth, giving you
grace to confess that Jesus Christ is Lord, and to proclaim
the wonderful works of God; and the blessing of God
Almighty, the Father, the Son, and the Holy Spirit, be among
you, and remain with you always. *Amen.*

The First Sunday after Pentecost: Trinity Sunday

The Lord bless you and keep you. *Amen.*

The Lord make his face to shine upon you, and be gracious to you. *Amen.*

The Lord lift up his countenance upon you, and give you peace. *Amen.*

The Lord God Almighty, Father, Son, and Holy Spirit, the holy and undivided Trinity, guard you, save you, and bring you to that heavenly City, where he lives and reigns for ever and ever. *Amen.*

or this

May God the Holy Trinity make you strong in faith and love, defend you on every side, and guide you in truth and peace; and the blessing of God Almighty, the Father, the Son, and the Holy Spirit, be among you, and remain with you always. *Amen.*

All Saints

May Almighty God, to whose glory we celebrate this festival of all the Saints, be now and evermore your guide and companion in the way. *Amen.*

May God, who has bound us together in the company of the elect, in this age and the age to come, attend to the prayers of his faithful servants on your behalf, as he hears your prayers for them. *Amen.*

May God, who has given us, in the lives of his saints, patterns of holy living and victorious dying, strengthen your faith and devotion, and enable you to bear witness to the truth against all adversity. *Amen.*

And the blessing of God Almighty, the Father, the Son, and the Holy Spirit, be upon you and remain with you for ever. *Amen.*

The preceding blessing may be adapted for use at a Patronal Festival.

or this

May God give you grace to follow his saints in faith and hope and love; and the blessing of God Almighty, the Father, the Son, and the Holy Spirit, be among you, and remain with you always. *Amen.*

Concerning the Advent Wreath

The Advent Wreath is a visual symbol marking the progress of the season of Advent. When it used in the church, no special prayers or ceremonial elaboration beyond what is described on page 143 of the Prayer Book is desirable. At morning services the appropriate number of candles is lighted before the service begins.

When used in private homes, the Advent Wreath provides a convenient focus for devotions at the time of the evening meal. The short form of An Order of Worship for the Evening, Prayer Book pages 109-112, is recommended.

In place of the Short Lesson of Scripture provided in the Order, one of the readings from the Daily Office Lectionary may be used, in whole or in part. Alternatively, some other plan of Bible reading may be followed.

Phos hilaron is always appropriate but an Advent hymn may be substituted for it.

Advent Festival
of Lessons and Music

The following bidding and lessons may be used at a festival held in Advent.

If the festival takes place in the evening, it may be introduced by the Service of Light (Prayer Book, page 109). The seasonal Lucernarium (page 12) or Psalm 85:7-13 may be sung during the candle lighting. After the Phos hilaron or the hymn sung in place of it, the service continues with the Bidding Prayer.

A Bidding Prayer   *Traditional*

Beloved in Christ, in this season of Advent, let it be our care and delight to prepare ourselves to hear again the message of the Angels, and in heart and mind to go even unto Bethlehem, to see the Babe lying in a manger.

Let us read and mark in Holy Scripture the tale of the loving purposes of God from the first days of our disobedience unto the glorious Redemption brought us by his holy Child; and let us look forward to the yearly remembrance of his birth with hymns and songs of praise.

But first, let us pray for the needs of his whole world; for peace and goodwill over all the earth; for the mission and unity of the Church for which he died, and especially in this country and within this *city*.

And because this of all things would rejoice his heart, let us at this time remember in his name the poor and the helpless; the hungry and the oppressed; the sick and those who mourn; the lonely and the unloved; the aged and the little children; and all those who know not the Lord Jesus, or who love him not, or who by sin have grieved his heart of love.

Lastly, let us remember before God his pure and lowly Mother, and all those who rejoice with us, but upon another shore and in a greater light, that multitude which no one can number, whose hope was in the Word made flesh, and with whom, in this Lord Jesus, we for evermore are one.

These prayers and praises let us humbly offer up to the throne of heaven, in the words which Christ himself hath taught us:

Our Father . . . .

The Almighty God bless us with his grace; Christ give us the joys of everlasting life; and unto the fellowship of the citizens above may the King of Angels bring us all. *Amen.*

A Bidding Prayer   *Contemporary*

Dear People of God: In the season of Advent, it is our responsibility and joy to prepare ourselves to hear once more the message of the Angels, to go to Bethlehem and see the Son of God lying in a manger.

Let us hear and heed in Holy Scripture the story of God's]loving purpose from the time of our rebellion against him until the glorious redemption brought to us by his holy Child Jesus, and let us look forward to the yearly remembrance of his birth with hymns and songs of praise.

But first, let us pray for the needs of his whole world, for peace and justice on earth, for the unity and mission of the Church for which he died, and especially for his Church in our country and in this *city.*

And because he particularly loves them, let us remember in his name the poor and helpless, the cold, the hungry and the oppressed, the sick and those who mourn, the lonely and unloved, the aged and little children, as well as all those who do not know and love the Lord Jesus Christ.

Finally, let us remember before God his pure and lowly Mother, and that whole multitude which no one can number, whose hope was in the Word made flesh, and with whom, in Jesus, we are one for evermore.

And now, to sum up all these petitions, let us pray in the words which Christ himself has taught us, saying:

Our Father . . . .

The Almighty God bless us with his grace; Christ give us the joys of everlasting life; and to the fellowship of the citizens above may the King of Angels bring us all. *Amen.*

The Lessons

Nine Lessons are customarily selected (but fewer may be used), interspersed with appropriate Advent hymns, canticles, and anthems. When possible, each Lesson is read by a different lector. The Lesson from the third chapter of Genesis is never omitted.

The Lessons may be read without announcement or conclusion, or in the manner prescribed in the Daily Office. A period of silence may follow each Lesson.

Genesis 2:4b-9,15-25 (God creates man and woman to live in obedience to him in the Garden of Eden)

Genesis 3:1-22 *or* 3:1-15 (Adam and Eve rebel against God and are cast out of the Garden of Eden)

Isaiah 40:1-11 (God comforts his people and calls on them to prepare for redemption)

Jeremiah 31:31-34 (A new covenant is promised which will be written in our hearts)

Isaiah 64:1-9a (God is called upon to act and to come among us)

Isaiah 6:1-11 (God reveals his glory to the prophet and calls him to be his messenger)

Isaiah 35:1-10 (The prophet proclaims that God will come and save us)

Baruch 4:36—5:9 (The Scribe Baruch urges the people to look East because salvation is at hand)

Isaiah 7:10-15 (God promises that a child shall be conceived who will be known as "God with us")

Micah 5:2-4 (The one who is to rule Israel will be born in the village of Bethlehem)

Isaiah 11:1-9 (The Spirit of the Lord will rest upon the Holy One)

Zephaniah 3:14-18 (The Lord will be among us; we are summoned to rejoice and sing)

Isaiah 65:17-25 (God promises a new heaven and a new earth)

If it is desired that the Lessons end with a reading from the Gospel, one of the following may be used:

Luke 1:5-25 (An angel announces to Zechariah that his wife Elizabeth will bear a son)

Luke 1:26-38 *or* 1:26-56 (The Angel Gabriel announces to the Virgin Mary that she will bear the Son of the Most High)

The service may conclude with an appropriate Collect and the seasonal blessing for Advent.

A sermon is not a traditional part of this service.

Vigil for Christmas Eve

If it is desired to preface the midnight Eucharist of Christmas by a vigil, the following form may be used.

The rite begins with the Service of Light, page 109 of the Prayer Book, using the Collect of the First Sunday after Christmas Day as the Prayer for Light. During the candle lighting, the seasonal Lucernarium (page 12) or Psalm 113 may be sung. The Magnificat or a suitable hymn, such as "Of the Father's love begotten," may be substituted for Phos hilaron.

After the hymn, a series of biblical passages is read (see pages 40-41 for suggestions), interspersed with anthems, canticles, hymns, carols, or instrumental music. A period of silent reflection may follow each Reading.

After the last reading, there may be a procession to the creche, where a suitable prayer is said.(See the next page.)

The procession then continues to the chancel, and the Eucharist begins in the usual way.

Station at a Christmas Creche

At their entry into the church for the celebration of the Holy Eucharist, the Celebrant (and other ministers) may make a station at a Christmas Creche. The figure of the Christ Child may be carried in the procession and placed in the creche. Other figures may also be brought in if desired.

A versicle may be said, and one of the prayers which follow.

V. The word was made flesh and dwelt among us:
R. And we beheld his glory.

or this

V. The glory of the Lord has been revealed:
R. And all flesh shall see the salvation of our God.

Let us pray.

Almighty and everliving God, you have given us a new revelation of your loving providence in the Coming of your Son Jesus Christ to be born of the Virgin Mary: Grant that as he shared our mortality, so we may share his eternity in the glory of your kingdom; where he lives and reigns for ever and ever. *Amen.*

or the following

O God our Creator, to restore our fallen race you spoke the effectual word, and the Eternal Word became flesh in the womb of the Blessed Virgin Mary: Mercifully grant that as he humbled himself to be clothed with our humanity, so we may be found worthy, in him, to be clothed with his divinity; who lives and reigns for ever and ever. *Amen.*

or this

Most merciful and loving God, you have made this day holy by the incarnation of your Son Jesus Christ, and by the child-bearing of the Blessed Virgin Mary: Grant that we your people may enter with joy into the celebration of this day, and may also rejoice for ever as your adopted sons and daughters; through Jesus Christ our Lord. *Amen.*

Any of the Collects for Christmas Season may be used instead.

Christmas Festival of Lessons and Music

The following bidding and lessons may be used at a festival during the Twelve Days of Christmas.

If the festival takes place in the evening, it may be introduced by the Service of Light (Prayer Book, page 109). The seasonal Lucernarium (page 12) or Psalm 113 may be sung during the candle lighting. After the Phos hilaron or the hymn sung in place of it, the service continues with the Bidding Prayer.

A Bidding Prayer *Traditional*

Beloved in Christ, in this Christmastide, let it be our care and delight to hear again the message of the Angels, and in heart and mind to go even unto Bethlehem, and see this thing which is come to pass, and the Babe lying in a manger.

Let us read and mark in Holy Scripture the tale of the loving purposes of God from the first days of our disobedience unto the glorious Redemption brought us by this holy Child; and let us make this *place* glad with our carols of praise.

But first, let us pray for the needs of his whole world; for peace and goodwill over all the earth; for the mission and unity of the Church for which he died, and especially in this country and within this *city*.

And because this of all things would rejoice his heart, let us at this time remember in his name the poor and the helpless, the hungry and the oppressed; the sick and those who mourn; the lonely and the unloved; the aged and the little children; and all those who know not the Lord Jesus, or who love him not, or who by sin have grieved his heart of love.

Lastly, let us remember before God his pure and lowly Mother, and all those who rejoice with us, but upon another shore and in a greater light, that multitude which no one can number, whose hope was in the Word made flesh, and with whom, in this Lord Jesus, we for evermore are one.

These prayers and praises let us humbly offer up to the throne of heaven, in the words which Christ himself hath taught us:

Our Father . . . .

The Almighty God bless us with his grace; Christ give us the joys of everlasting life; and unto the fellowship of the citizens above may the King of Angels bring us all. *Amen.*

A Bidding Prayer   *Contemporary*

Dear People of God: In this Christmas Season, let it be our duty and delight to hear once more the message of the Angels, to go to Bethlehem and see the Son of God lying in a manger.

Let us hear and heed in Holy Scripture the story of God's loving purpose from the time of our rebellion against him until the glorious redemption brought to us by his holy Child Jesus, and let us make this *place* glad with our carols of praise.

But first, let us pray for the needs of his whole world, for peace and justice on earth, for the unity and mission of the Church for which he died, and especially for his Church in our country and in this *city*.

And because he particularly loves them, let us remember in his name the poor and helpless, the cold, the hungry and the oppressed, the sick and those who mourn, the lonely and unloved, the aged and little children, as well as all those who do not know and love the Lord Jesus Christ.

Finally, let us remember before God his pure and lowly Mother, and that whole multitude which no one can number, whose hope was in the Word made flesh, and with whom, in Jesus, we are one for evermore.

And now, to sum up all these petitions, let us pray in the words which Christ himself has taught us, saying:

Our Father . . . .

The Almighty God bless us with his grace; Christ give us the joys of everlasting life; and to the fellowship of the citizens above, may the King of Angels bring us all. *Amen.*

The Lessons

Nine Lessons are customarily selected (but fewer may be used), interspersed with appropriate carols, hymns, canticles, and anthems. When possible, each lesson is read by a different lector. The lesson from the third chapter of Genesis is never omitted.

The Lessons may be read without announcement or conclusion, or in the manner prescribed in the Daily Office.

Genesis 2:4b-9,15-25 (God creates man and woman to live in obedience to him in the Garden of Eden)
Genesis 3:1-23 or 3:1-15 (Adam and Eve rebel against God and are cast out of the Garden of Eden)

Isaiah 40:1-11 (God comforts his people and calls on them to prepare for redemption)

Isaiah 35:1-10 (The prophet proclaims that God will come and save us)

Isaiah 7:10-15 (God promises that a child shall be conceived who will be known as "God with us")

Luke 1:5-25 (An angel announces to Zechariah that his wife Elizabeth will bear a son)

Luke 1:26-58 (The Angel Gabriel announces to the Virgin Mary that she will bear the Son of the Most High)

Luke 1:39-46 or 1:39-56 (The Virgin Mary is greeted by Elizabeth and proclaims her joy)

Luke 1:57-80 (John the Baptist is born and his father rejoices that his son will prepare the way of the Lord)

Luke 2:1-20 (Jesus is born at Bethlehem and is worshiped by angels and shepherds)

Luke 2:21-36 (Jesus receives his name and is presented to Simeon in the Temple)

Hebrews 1:1-12 (In the fullness of time, God sent his Son whose reign is for ever and ever)

John 1:1-18 (The Word was made flesh and we have seen his glory)

The service may conclude with a suitable Collect and the seasonal blessing for Christmas.

A sermon is not a traditional part of this service.

Service for New Year's Eve

During the evening of December 31, which is the eve of the Feast of the Holy Name and also the eve of the civil New Year, the following service may be used.

The rite begins with the Service of Light, page 109 of the Prayer Book, using the Collect for the First Sunday after Christmas as the Prayer for Light.

After the Phos hilaron, two or more of the following Lessons are read, each followed by a Psalm, Canticle, or hymn, and a Prayer. The last reading is always from the New Testament.

The Hebrew Year
Exodus 23:9-16,20-21

Psalm 111,   *or*   Psalm 119:1-8

Let us pray.   *(Silence)*

O God our Creator, you have divided our life into days and seasons, and called us to acknowledge your providence year after year: Accept your people who come to offer their praises, and, in your mercy, receive their prayers; through Jesus Christ our Lord. *Amen.*

The Promised Land
Deuteronomy 11:8-12,26-28

Psalm 36:5-10, *or* Psalm 89, Part I

Let us pray. *(Silence)*

Almighty God, the source of all life, giver of all blessing, and savior of all who turn to you: Have mercy upon this nation; deliver us from falsehood, malice, and disobedience; turn our feet into your paths; and grant that we may serve you in peace; through Jesus Christ our Lord. *Amen.*

A Season for all Things
Ecclesiastes 3:1-15

Psalm 90

Let us pray. *(Silence)*

In your wisdom, O Lord our God, you have made all things, and have allotted to each of us the days of our life: Grant that we may live in your presence, be guided by your Holy Spirit, and offer all our works to your honor and glory; through Jesus Christ our Lord. *Amen.*

Remember your Creator
Ecclesiastes 12:1-8

Psalm 130

Let us pray. *(Silence)*

Immortal Lord God, you inhabit eternity, and have brought us your unworthy servants to the close of another year: Pardon, we entreat you, our transgressions of the past, and graciously abide with us all the days of our life; through Jesus Christ our Lord. *Amen.*

Marking the Times, and Winter
Ecclesiasticus 43:1-22

Psalm 19, *or* Psalm 148, *or* Psalm 74:11-22

Let us pray. *(Silence)*

Almighty Father, you give the sun for a light by day, and the moon and the stars by night: Graciously receive us, this night and always, into your favor and protection, defending us from all harm and governing us with your Holy Spirit, that every shadow of ignorance, every failure of faith or weakness of heart, every evil or wrong desire may be removed far from us; so that we, being justified in our Lord Jesus Christ, may be sanctified by your Spirit, and glorified by your infinite mercies in the day of the glorious appearing of our Lord and Savior Jesus Christ. *Amen.*

The Acceptable Time
2 Corinthians 5:17—6:2

Psalm 63:1-8, *or* Canticle 5 *or* Canticle 17

Let us pray. *(Silence)*

Most gracious and merciful God, you have reconciled us to yourself through Jesus Christ your Son, and called us to new life in him: Grant that we, who begin this year in his Name, may complete it to his honor and glory; who lives and reigns now and for ever. *Amen.*

While it is Called Today
Hebrews 3:1-15 (16—4:13)

Psalm 95

Let us pray.   *(Silence)*

O God, through your Son you have taught us to be watchful, and to await the sudden day of judgment: Strengthen us against Satan and his forces of wickedness, the evil powers of this world, and the sinful desires within us; and grant that, having served you all the days of our life, we may finally come to the dwelling place your Son has prepared for us; who lives and reigns for ever and ever. *Amen.*

New Heavens and New Earth
Revelation 21:1-14,22-24

Canticle 19

Let us pray.   *(Silence)*

Almighty and merciful God, through your well beloved Son Jesus Christ, the King of kings and Lord of lords, you have willed to make all things new: Grant that we may be renewed by your Holy Spirit, and may come at last to that heavenly country where your people hunger and thirst no more, and the tears are wiped away from every eye; through Jesus Christ our Lord. *Amen.*

A homily, sermon, or instruction may follow the Readings.

An act of self-dedication may follow.

The service may conclude in one of the following ways:

1. With the recitation of the Great Litany or some other form of intercession.

2. With the singing of Te Deum laudamus or some other hymn of praise, followed by the Lord's Prayer, the Collect for Holy Name, and a blessing or dismissal, or both.

3. With the Eucharist, beginning with the Gloria in excelsis or some other song of praise. The Proper for the Feast of the Holy Name is used.

Blessing in Homes
at Epiphany

Where it is customary to invite the parish priest to the homes of parishioners on the Feast of the Epiphany or during the week following, this blessing may be used.

The Celebrant begins with the following or some other greeting

Peace be to this house, and to all who dwell in it.

The Magnificat is then sung or said with one of the following antiphons:

The Lord has shown forth his glory: Come let us adore him.

or this

I saw water proceeding out of the temple; from the right side it flowed, alleluia; and all those to whom that water came shall be saved, and shall say, alleluia, alleluia.

My soul proclaims the greatness of the Lord,
my spirit rejoices in God my Savior; *
    for he has looked with favor on his lowly servant
From this day all generations will call me blessed: *
    the Almighty has done great things for me,
    and holy is his Name.
He has mercy on those who fear him *
    in every generation.

He has shown the strength of his arm, *
   he has scattered the proud in their conceit.
He has cast down the mighty from their thrones, *
   and has lifted up the lowly.
He has filled the hungry with good things, *
   and the rich he has sent away empty.
He has come to the help of his servant Israel, *
   for he has remembered his promise of mercy,
The promise he made to our fathers, *
   to Abraham and his children for ever.
Glory to the Father, and to the Son, and to the Holy Spirit: *
   as it was in the beginning, is now, and will be for ever. Amen.

The antiphon is then repeated.

Celebrant	The Lord be with you.
People	And also with you.
Celebrant	Let us pray.

The Celebrant says one of the following Collects:

O God, by the leading of a star you manifested your only
Son to the peoples of the earth: Lead us, who know you now
by faith, to your presence, where we may see your glory face
to face; through Jesus Christ our Lord, who lives and reigns
with you and the Holy Spirit, one God, now and for
ever. *Amen.*

or this

Father in heaven, who at the baptism of Jesus in the River
Jordan proclaimed him your beloved Son and anointed him
with the Holy Spirit: Grant that all who are baptized into his
Name may keep the covenant they have made, and boldly
confess him as Lord and Savior; who with you and the Holy
Spirit lives and reigns, one God, in glory everlasting. *Amen.*

The Celebrant then says this prayer

Visit, O blessed Lord, this home with the gladness of your presence, Bless *all* who *live* here with the gift of your love; and grant that *they* may manifest your love [to each other and] to all whose lives *they touch*. May *they* grow in grace and in the knowledge and love of you; guide, comfort, and strengthen *them*; and preserve *them* in peace, O Jesus Christ, now and for ever. *Amen.*

Other suitable prayers may be added.

The Celebrant may say one of the two following blessings:

May God the Father, who by Baptism adopts us as his children, grant you grace. *Amen.*

May God the Son, who sanctified a home at Nazareth, fill you with love. *Amen.*
May God the Holy Spirit, who has made the Church one family, keep you in peace. *Amen.*

or this

May Almighty God, who led the Wise Men by the shining of a star to find the Christ, the Light from Light, lead you also in your pilgrimage, to find the Lord. *Amen.*

May God, who sent the Holy Spirit to rest upon the Only-begotten at his baptism in the Jordan River, pour out that Spirit on you who have come to the waters of new birth. *Amen.*

May God, by the power that turned water into wine at the wedding feast at Cana, transform your lives and make glad your hearts. *Amen.*

And the blessing of God Almighty, the Father, the Son, and the Holy Spirit, be upon you and remain with you for ever. *Amen.*

The Peace may then be exchanged.

Vigil for the Eve
of the Baptism of Our Lord

*When a Vigil of the Baptism of the Lord is observed, it begins with the
Service of Light, page 109 of the Prayer Book (substituting, if desired,
the Gloria in excelsis for the Phos hilaron), and continues with the
Salutation and Collect of the Day. Three or more Lessons are read before
the Gospel, each followed by a period of silence and a Psalm, Canticle,
or hymn. Holy Baptism or Confirmation (beginning with the
Presentation of the Candidates), or the Renewal of Baptismal Vows,
Prayer Book page 292, follows the Sermon.*

The Story of the Flood
Genesis (7:1-5,11-18); 8:6-18; 9:8-13

Psalm 25:3-9,   *or*   Psalm 46

The Lord who Makes a Way in the Sea
Isaiah 43:15-19

Psalm 114

The Washing and Anointing of Aaron
Leviticus 8:1-12

Psalm 23   *or*   Psalm 133

The Anointing of David
1 Samuel 16:1-13

Psalm 2:1-8   *or*   Psalm 110:1-5

The Cleansing of Naaman in the Jordan
2 Kings 5:1-14

Psalm 51:8-13

Salvation Offered Freely to All
Isaiah 55:1-11

Canticle 9, The First Song of Isaiah

A new Heart and a new Spirit
Ezekiel 36:24-28

Psalm 42

The Spirit of the Lord is Upon Me
Isaiah 61:1-9

or   **Behold my Servant ***
     Isaiah 42:1-9

Psalm 89:20-29*

When God's Patience Waited in the Days of Noah
1 Peter 3:15b-22

or   **God Anointed Jesus with the Holy Spirit ***
     Acts 10:34-38

The Baptism of Jesus *
Year A: Matthew 3:13-17
Year B: Mark 1:7-11
Year C: Luke 3:15-16,21-22

or   **The Resurrection and the Great Commission**
     Matthew 28:1-10,16-20

*Proper Readings and Psalm for the Eucharist of the Feast

Candlemas Procession

This procession is intended for use immediately before the Holy Eucharist on the Feast of the Presentation of Our Lord in the Temple.

When circumstances permit, the congregation gathers at a place apart from the church so that all may go into the church in procession. If necessary, however, the procession takes place within the church. In this case it is suitable that the celebrant begin the rite standing just inside the door of the church.

All are provided with unlighted candles. A server holds the celebrant's candle until the procession begins. The congregation stands facing the celebrant.

The Celebrant greets the people with these words

Light and peace, in Jesus Christ our Lord.
People   Thanks be to God.

The following canticle is then sung or said, during which the candles are lighted.

A Light to enlighten the nations,
and the glory of your people Israel.
A Light to enlighten the nations,
and the glory of your people Israel.

Lord, you now have set your servant free *
　to go in peace as you have promised.
A Light to enlighten the nations,
and the glory of your people Israel.

For these eyes of mine have seen the Savior, *
　whom you have prepared for all the world to see.
A Light to enlighten the nations,
and the glory of your people Israel.

The Celebrant then says the following prayer

Let us pray.

God our Father, source of all light, today you revealed to the aged Simeon your light which enlightens the nations. Fill our hearts with the light of faith, that we who bear these candles may walk in the path of goodness, and come to the Light that shines for ever, your Son Jesus Christ our Lord. *Amen.*

The Procession

Deacon　　Let us go forth in peace.
People　　In the name of Christ. Amen.

During the procession, all carry lighted candles; and appropriate hymns, psalms, or anthems are sung.

At a suitable place, the procession may halt while the following or some other appropriate Collect is said

Let us pray.

O God, you have made this day holy by the presentation of your Son in the Temple, and by the purification of the Blessed Virgin Mary: Mercifully grant that we, who delight in her humble readiness to be the birth-giver of the Only-begotten, may rejoice for ever in our adoption as his sisters and brothers; through Jesus Christ our Lord. *Amen.*

The following antiphon and psalm is appropriate as the procession approaches the Altar

We have waited in silence on your loving-kindness, O Lord, in the midst of your temple. Your praise, like your Name, O God, reaches to the world's end; your right hand is full of justice.

Psalm 48:1-2,10-13

In place of the long antiphon given above, this shorter form may be used with the appointed Psalm

We have waited on your loving-kindness, O Lord, in the midst of your temple.

On arrival in the sanctuary, the celebrant goes to the usual place, and the Eucharist begins with the Gloria in excelsis.

After the Collect of the Day, all extinguish their candles.

If desired, the candles of the congregation may be lighted again at the time of the dismissal, and borne by them as they leave the church.

Concerning the Service

The devotion known as the Way of the Cross is an adaptation to local usage of a custom widely observed by pilgrims to Jerusalem: the offering of prayer at a series of places in that city traditionally associated with our Lord's passion and death.

The number of stations, which at first varied widely, finally became fixed at fourteen. Of these, eight are based directly on events recorded in the Gospels. The remaining six (numbers 3, 4, 6, 7, 9, and 13) are based on inferences from the Gospel account or from pious legend. If desired, these six stations may be omitted.

The form which follows is appropriate either as a public service or as a private devotion, particularly on the Fridays of Lent, but it should not displace the Proper Liturgy of Good Friday.

Traditionally, the stations are made before a series of plain wooden crosses placed along the walls of the church or in some other convenient place. With each cross there is sometimes associated a pictorial representation of the event being commemorated.

The hymn Stabat Mater ("At the cross her station keeping") has frequently been associated with this service, but is not an integral part of it. Selected stanzas of this hymn may appropriately be sung at the entrance of the ministers, and (after the opening devotions before the Altar) as the procession approaches the first station.

In the form which follows, the Trisagion ("Holy God") is the chant recommended as the procession goes from station to station. Alternatively, the Trisagion may be used to conclude each station, and stanzas of appropriate hymns sung as the procession moves. It is appropriate that all present take part in the procession.

The officiant at the service, whether clerical or lay, customarily leads the opening versicle at each station and reads the concluding Collect. The Readings (and the versicles which follow) are appropriately assigned to other persons.

The Way of the Cross

A hymn or other song may be sung during the entrance of the ministers.

Opening Devotions

In the Name of the Father, and of the Son, and of the Holy
Spirit. *Amen.*

Lord, have mercy.
Christ, have mercy.
Lord, have mercy.

Officiant and People

Our Father, who art in heaven,
 hallowed be thy Name,
 thy kingdom come,
 thy will be done,
  on earth as it is in heaven.
Give us this day our daily bread.
And forgive us our trespasses,
 as we forgive those
  who trespass against us.
And lead us not into temptation,
 but deliver us from evil.

Our Father in heaven,
 hallowed be your Name,
 your kingdom come,
 your will be done
  on earth as in heaven.
Give us today our daily bread.
Forgive us our sins
 as we forgive those
  who sin against us.
Save us from the time of trial,
 and deliver us from evil.

V. We will glory in the cross of our Lord Jesus Christ:
R. In whom is our salvation, our life and resurrection.

Let us pray. *(Silence)*

Assist us mercifully with your help, O Lord God of our salvation, that we may enter with joy upon the contemplation of those mighty acts, whereby you have given us life and immortality; through Jesus Christ our Lord. *Amen.*

The procession goes to the First Station.

First Station

Jesus is condemned to death

We adore you, O Christ, and we bless you:
Because by your holy cross you have redeemed the world.

As soon as it was morning, the chief priests, with the elders and scribes, and the whole council, held a consultation; and they bound Jesus and led him away and delivered him to Pilate. And they all condemned him and said, "He deserves to die." When Pilate heard these words, he brought Jesus out and sat down on the judgment seat at a place called the Pavement, but in the Hebrew, Gabbatha. Then he handed Jesus over to them to be crucified.

V. God did not spare his own Son:
R. But delivered him up for us all.

Let us pray.   *(Silence)*

Almighty God, whose most dear Son went not up to joy but first he suffered pain, and entered not into glory before he was crucified: Mercifully grant that we, walking in the way of the cross, may find it none other than the way of life and peace; through Jesus Christ your Son our Lord. *Amen.*

Holy God,
Holy and Mighty,
Holy Immortal One,
Have mercy upon us.

Second Station

Jesus takes up his Cross

We adore you, O Christ, and we bless you:
Because by your holy cross you have redeemed the world.

Jesus went out, bearing his own cross, to the place called the place of a skull, which is called in Hebrew, Golgotha. Although he was a Son, he learned obedience through what he suffered. Like a lamb he was led to the slaughter; and like a sheep that before its shearers is mute, so he opened not his mouth. Worthy is the Lamb who was slain, to receive power and riches and wisdom and strength and honor and glory and blessing.

V. The Lord has laid on him the iniquity of us all:
R. For the transgression of my people was he stricken.

Let us pray. *(Silence)*

Almighty God, whose beloved Son willingly endured the agony and shame of the cross for our redemption: Give us courage to take up our cross and follow him; who lives and reigns for ever and ever. *Amen.*

Holy God,
Holy and Mighty,
Holy Immortal One,
Have mercy upon us.

Third Station

Jesus falls the first time

We adore you, O Christ, and we bless you:
Because by your holy cross you have redeemed the world.

Christ Jesus, though he was in the form of God, did not count equality with God a thing to be grasped; but emptied himself, taking the form of a servant, and was born in human likeness. And being found in human form he humbled himself and became obedient unto death, even death on a cross. Therefore God has highly exalted him, and bestowed on him the name which is above every name. Come, let us bow down, and bend the knee, and kneel before the Lord our Maker, for he is the Lord our God.

V. Surely he has borne our griefs:
R. And carried our sorrows.

Let us pray. *(Silence)*

O God, you know us to be set in the midst of so many and great dangers, that by reason of the frailty of our nature we cannot always stand upright: Grant us such strength and protection as may support us in all dangers, and carry us through all temptations; through Jesus Christ our Lord. *Amen.*

Holy God,
Holy and Mighty,
Holy Immortal One,
Have mercy upon us.

Fourth Station

Jesus meets his afflicted mother

We adore you, O Christ, and we bless you:
Because by your holy cross you have redeemed the world.

To what can I liken you, to what can I compare you, O
daughter of Jerusalem? What likeness can I use to comfort
you, O virgin daughter of Zion? For vast as the sea is your
ruin. Blessed are those who mourn, for they shall be
comforted. The Lord will be your everlasting light, and your
days of mourning shall be ended.

V.   A sword will pierce your own soul also:
R.   And fill your heart with bitter pain.

Let us pray.   *(Silence)*

O God, who willed that in the passion of your Son a sword
of grief should pierce the soul of the Blessed Virgin Mary his
mother: Mercifully grant that your Church, having shared
with her in his passion, may be made worthy to share in the
joys of his resurrection; who lives and reigns for ever and
ever. *Amen.*

Holy God,
Holy and Mighty,
Holy Immortal One,
Have mercy upon us.

Fifth Station

The Cross is laid on Simon of Cyrene

We adore you, O Christ, and we bless you:
Because by your holy cross you have redeemed the world.

As they led Jesus away, they came upon a man of Cyrene, Simon by name, who was coming in from the country, and laid on him the cross to carry it behind Jesus. "If anyone would come after me, let him deny himself and take up his cross and follow me. Take my yoke upon you, and learn from me; for my yoke is easy, and my burden is light."

V. Whoever does not bear his own cross and come after me:
R. Cannot be my disciple.

Let us pray. *(Silence)*

Heavenly Father, whose blessed Son came not to be served but to serve: Bless all who, following in his steps, give themselves to the service of others; that with wisdom, patience, and courage, they may minister in his Name to the suffering, the friendless, and the needy; for the love of him who laid down his life for us, your Son our Savior Jesus Christ. *Amen.*

Holy God,
Holy and Mighty,
Holy Immortal One,
Have mercy upon us.

Sixth Station

A woman wipes the face of Jesus

We adore you, O Christ, and we bless you:
Because by your holy cross you have redeemed the world.

We have seen him without beauty or majesty, with no looks to attract our eyes. He was despised and rejected by men; a man of sorrows, and acquainted with grief; and as one from whom men hide their faces, he was despised, and we esteemed him not. His appearance was so marred, beyond human semblance, and his form beyond that of the children of men. But he was wounded for our transgressions, he was bruised for our iniquities; upon him was the chastisement that made us whole, and with his stripes we are healed.

V.   Restore us, O Lord God of hosts:
R.   Show the light of your countenance, and we shall be saved.

Let us pray.   *(Silence)*

O God, who before the passion of your only-begotten Son revealed his glory upon the holy mountain: Grant to us that we, beholding by faith the light of his countenance, may be strengthened to bear our cross, and be changed into his likeness from glory to glory; through Jesus Christ our Lord. *Amen.*

Holy God,
Holy and Mighty,
Holy Immortal One,
Have mercy upon us.

Seventh Station

Jesus falls a second time

We adore you, O Christ, and we bless you:
Because by your holy cross you have redeemed the world.

Surely he has borne our griefs and carried our sorrows. All
we like sheep have gone astray; we have turned every one to
his own way; and the Lord has laid on him the iniquity of us
all. He was oppressed, and he was afflicted, yet he opened
not his mouth. For the transgression of my people was he
stricken.

V. But as for me, I am a worm and no man:
R. Scorned by all and despised by the people.

Let us pray. *(Silence)*

Almighty and everliving God, in your tender love for the
human race you sent your Son our Savior Jesus Christ to
take upon him our nature, and to suffer death upon the
cross, giving us the example of his great humility: Mercifully
grant that we may walk in the way of his suffering, and also
share in his resurrection; who lives and reigns for ever and
ever. *Amen.*

Holy God,
Holy and Mighty,
Holy Immortal One,
Have mercy upon us.

Eighth Station

Jesus meets the women of Jerusalem

We adore you, O Christ, and we bless you:
Because by your holy cross you have redeemed the world.

There followed after Jesus a great multitude of the people, and among them were women who bewailed and lamented him. But Jesus turning to them said, "Daughters of Jerusalem, do not weep for me, but weep for yourselves and for your children."

V. Those who sowed with tears:
R. Will reap with songs of joy.

Let us pray. *(Silence)*

Teach your Church, O Lord, to mourn the sins of which it is guilty, and to repent and forsake them; that, by your pardoning grace, the results of our iniquities may not be visited upon our children and our children's children; through Jesus Christ our Lord. *Amen.*

Holy God,
Holy and Mighty,
Holy Immortal One,
Have mercy upon us.

Ninth Station

Jesus falls a third time

We adore you, O Christ, and we bless you:
Because by your holy cross you have redeemed the world.

I am the man who has seen affliction under the rod of his wrath; he has driven and brought me into darkness without any light. He has besieged me and enveloped me with bitterness and tribulation; he has made me dwell in darkness like the dead of long ago. Though I call and cry for help, he shuts out my prayer. He has made my teeth grind on gravel, and made me cower in ashes. "Remember, O Lord, my affliction and bitterness, the wormwood and the gall!"

V. He was led like a lamb to the slaughter:
R. And like a sheep that before its shearers is mute, so he opened not his mouth.

Let us pray. *(Silence)*

O God, by the passion of your blessed Son you made an instrument of shameful death to be for us the means of life: Grant us so to glory in the cross of Christ, that we may gladly suffer shame and loss for the sake of your Son our Savior Jesus Christ. *Amen.*

Holy God,
Holy and Mighty,
Holy Immortal One,
Have mercy upon us.

Tenth Station

Jesus is stripped of his garments

We adore you, O Christ, and we bless you:
Because by your holy cross you have redeemed the world.

When they came to a place called Golgotha (which means the place of a skull), they offered him wine to drink, mingled with gall; but when he tasted it, he would not drink it. And they divided his garments among them by casting lots. This was to fulfill the scripture which says, "They divided my garments among them; they cast lots for my clothing."

V.   They gave me gall to eat:
R.   And when I was thirsty they gave me vinegar to drink.

Let us pray.   *(Silence)*

Lord God, whose blessed Son our Savior gave his body to be whipped and his face to be spit upon: Give us grace to accept joyfully the sufferings of the present time, confident of the glory that shall be revealed; through Jesus Christ our Lord. *Amen.*

Holy God,
Holy and Mighty,
Holy Immortal One,
Have mercy upon us.

Eleventh Station

Jesus is nailed to the Cross

We adore you, O Christ, and we bless you:
Because by your holy cross you have redeemed the world.

When they came to the place which is called The Skull, there they crucified him; and with him they crucified two criminals, one on the right, the other on the left, and Jesus between them. And the scripture was fulfilled which says, "He was numbered with the transgressors."

V. They pierce my hands and my feet:
R. They stare and gloat over me.

Let us pray. *(Silence)*

Lord Jesus Christ, you stretched out your arms of love on the hard wood of the cross that everyone might come within the reach of your saving embrace: So clothe us in your Spirit that we, reaching forth our hands in love, may bring those who do not know you to the knowledge and love of you; for the honor of your Name. *Amen.*

Holy God,
Holy and Mighty,
Holy Immortal One,
Have mercy upon us.

Twelfth Station

Jesus dies on the Cross

We adore you, O Christ, and we bless you:
Because by your holy cross you have redeemed the world.

When Jesus saw his mother, and the disciple whom he loved standing near, he said to his mother, "Woman, behold your son!" Then he said to the disciple, "Behold your mother!" And when Jesus had received the vinegar, he said, "It is finished!" And then, crying with a loud voice, he said, "Father, into your hands I commend my spirit." And he bowed his head, and handed over his spirit.

V. Christ for us became obedient unto death:
R. Even death on a cross.

Let us pray. *(Silence)*

O God, who for our redemption gave your only-begotten Son to the death of the cross, and by his glorious resurrection delivered us from the power of our enemy: Grant us so to die daily to sin, that we may evermore live with him in the joy of his resurrection; who lives and reigns now and for ever. *Amen.*

Holy God,
Holy and Mighty,
Holy Immortal One,
Have mercy upon us.

Thirteenth Station

The body of Jesus is placed in the arms of his mother

We adore you, O Christ, and we bless you:
Because by your holy cross you have redeemed the world.

All you who pass by, behold and see if there is any sorrow like my sorrow. My eyes are spent with weeping; my soul is in tumult; my heart is poured out in grief because of the downfall of my people. "Do not call me Naomi (which means Pleasant), call me Mara (which means Bitter); for the Almighty has dealt very bitterly with me."

V.   Her tears run down her cheeks:
R.   And she has none to comfort her.

Let us pray.   *(Silence)*

Lord Jesus Christ, by your death you took away the sting of death: Grant to us your servants so to follow in faith where you have led the way, that we may at length fall asleep peacefully in you and wake up in your likeness; for your tender mercies' sake. *Amen.*

Holy God,
Holy and Mighty,
Holy Immortal One,
Have mercy upon us.

Fourteenth Station

Jesus is laid in the tomb

We adore you, O Christ, and we bless you:
Because by your holy cross you have redeemed the world.

When it was evening, there came a rich man from
Arimathea, named Joseph, who also was a disciple of
Jesus. He went to Pilate and asked for the body of Jesus.
Then Pilate ordered it to be given to him. And Joseph took
the body, and wrapped it in a clean linen shroud, and laid it
in his own new tomb, which he had hewn in the rock; and
he rolled a great stone to the door of the tomb.

V. You will not abandon me to the grave:
R. Nor let your holy One see corruption.

Let us pray. *(Silence)*

O God, your blessed Son was laid in a tomb in a garden, and
rested on the Sabbath day: Grant that we who have been
buried with him in the waters of baptism may find our
perfect rest in his eternal and glorious kingdom; where he
lives and reigns for ever and ever. *Amen.*

Holy God,
Holy and Mighty,
Holy Immortal One,
Have mercy upon us.

Concluding Prayers before the Altar

Savior of the world, by your cross and precious blood you have redeemed us:
Save us, and help us, we humbly beseech you, O Lord.

Let us pray. *(Silence)*

We thank you, heavenly Father, that you have delivered us from the dominion of sin and death and brought us into the kingdom of your Son; and we pray that, as by his death he has recalled us to life, so by his love he may raise us to eternal joys; who lives and reigns with you, in the unity of the Holy Spirit, one God, now and for ever. *Amen.*

To Christ our Lord who loves us, and washed us in his own blood, and made us a kingdom of priests to serve his God and Father, to him be glory and dominion for ever and ever. *Amen.*

Concerning the Service

The name *Tenebrae* (the Latin word for "darkness" or "shadows") has for centuries been applied to the ancient monastic night and early morning services (Matins and Lauds) of the last three days of Holy Week, which in medieval times came to be celebrated on the preceding evenings.

Apart from the chant of the Lamentations (in which each verse is introduced by a letter of the Hebrew alphabet), the most conspicuous feature of the service is the gradual extinguishing of candles and other lights in the church until only a single candle, considered a symbol of our Lord, remains. Toward the end of the service this candle is hidden, typifying the apparent victory of the forces of evil. At the very end, a loud noise is made, symbolizing the earthquake at the time of the resurrection (Matthew 28:2), the hidden candle is restored to its place, and by its light all depart in silence.

In this book, provision is made for Tenebrae on Wednesday evening only, in order that the proper liturgies of Maundy Thursday and Good Friday may find their place as the principal services of those days. By drawing upon material from each of the former three offices of Tenebrae, this service provides an extended meditation upon, and a prelude to, the events in our Lord's life between the Last Supper and the Resurrection.

Additional Directions are on page 91.

Tenebrae

The ministers enter the church in silence and proceed to their places. The Office then begins immediately with the Antiphon on the first Psalm. It is customary to sit for the Psalmody.

First Nocturn

Antiphon 1

Zeal for your house has eaten me up; the scorn of those who scorn you has fallen upon me.

Psalm 69, or *Psalm 69:1-23*

Antiphon 2

Let them draw back and be disgraced who take pleasure in my misfortune.

Psalm 70

Antiphon 3

Arise, O God, maintain my cause.

Psalm 74

V. Deliver me, my God, from the hand of the wicked:
R. From the clutches of the evildoer and the oppressor.

All stand for silent prayer. The appointed Reader then goes to the lectern, and everyone else sits down.

Lesson 1

A Reading from the Lamentations of Jeremiah the Prophet. [1:1-14]

Aleph. How solitary lies the city, once so full of people! How like a widow has she become, she that was great among the nations! She that was queen among the cities has now become a vassal.

Beth. She weeps bitterly in the night, tears run down her cheeks; among all her lovers she has none to comfort her; all become her enemies.

Gimel. Judah has gone into the misery of exile and of hard servitude; she dwells now among the nations, but finds no resting place; all her pursuers overtook her in the midst of her anguish.

Daleth. The roads to Zion mourn, because none come to the solemn feasts; all her gates are desolate, her priests groan and sigh; her virgins are afflicted, and she is in bitterness.

He. Her adversaries have become her masters, her enemies prosper; because the Lord has punished her for the multitude of her rebellions; her children are gone, driven away as captives by the enemy.

Jerusalem, Jerusalem, return to the Lord your God!

Responsory 1 *In monte Oliveti*

On the mount of Olives Jesus prayed to the Father:
Father, if it be possible, let this cup pass from me.
The spirit indeed is willing, but the flesh is weak.
V.   Watch and pray, that you may not enter into temptation.
The spirit indeed is willing, but the flesh is weak.

Lesson 2

Waw. And from Daughter Zion all her majesty has departed;
her princes have become like stags that can find no pasture,
and that run without strength before the hunter.

Zayin. Jerusalem remembers in the days of her affliction and
bitterness all the precious things that were hers from the
days of old; when her people fell into the hand of the foe,
and there was none to help her; the adversary saw her, and
mocked at her downfall.

Heth. Jerusalem has sinned greatly, therefore she has become
a thing unclean; all who honored her despise her, for they
have seen her nakedness; and now she sighs, and turns her
face away.

Teth. Uncleanness clung to her skirts, she took no thought of
her doom; therefore her fall is terrible, she has no comforter.
"O Lord, behold my affliction, for the enemy has triumphed."

Jerusalem, Jerusalem, return to the Lord your God!

Responsory 2 *Tristis est anima mea*

My soul is very sorrowful, even to the point of death;
remain here, and watch with me.

Now you shall see the crowd who will surround me;
you will flee, and I will go to be offered up for you.
V.   Behold, the hour is at hand, and the Son of Man
     is betrayed into the hands of sinners.
You will flee, and I will go to be offered up for you

Lesson 3

Yodh. The adversary has stretched out his hand to seize all
her precious things; she has seen the Gentiles invade her
sanctuary, those whom you had forbidden to enter your
congregation.

Kaph. All her people groan as they search for bread; they sell
their own children for food to revive their strength. "Behold,
O Lord, and consider, for I am now beneath contempt!"

Lamedh. Is it nothing to you, all you who pass by? Behold
and see if there is any sorrow like my sorrow, which was
brought upon me, which the Lord inflicted, on the day of his
burning anger.

Mem. From on high he sent fire, into my bones it descended;
he spread a net for my feet, and turned me back; he has left
me desolate and faint all the day long.

Nun. My transgressions were bound into a yoke; by his
hand they were fastened together; their yoke is upon my
neck; he has caused my strength to fail. The Lord has
delivered me into their hands, against whom I am not able to
stand up.

Jerusalem, Jerusalem, return to the Lord your God!

Responsory 3 *Ecce vidimus eum*

Lo, we have seen him without beauty or majesty,
with no looks to attract our eyes.
He bore our sins and grieved for us,
he was wounded for our transgressions,
and by his scourging we are healed.
V. Surely he has borne our griefs and carried our sorrows:
And by his scourging we are healed.

When this Responsory is sung rather than recited, repeat all that
precedes the Verse:

Lo, we have seen . . . we are healed.

Second Nocturn

Antiphon 4

The kings of the earth rise up in revolt, and the princes plot
together, against the Lord and against his Anointed.

Psalm 2

Antiphon 5

They divide my garments among them; they cast lots for my
clothing.

Psalm 22, or Psalm 22:1-21

Antiphon 6

False witnesses have risen up against me, and also those who
speak malice.

Psalm 27

V. They divide my garments among them:
R. They cast lots for my clothing.

*All stand for silent prayer. The appointed Reader then goes to the
lectern, and everyone else sits down.*

Lesson 4

A Reading from the Treatise of Saint Augustine the Bishop on
the Psalms. [Vulgate Psalm 54. Prayer Book Psalm 55:1,2,10c]

Hear my prayer, O God; do not hide yourself from my
petition. Listen to me and answer me. I mourn in my trial
and am troubled."
These are the words of one disquieted, in trouble and
anxiety. He prays under much suffering, desiring to be
delivered from evil. Let us now see under what evil he lies;
and when he begins to speak, let us place ourselves beside
him, that, by sharing his tribulation, we may also join in his
prayer.

"I mourn in my trial," he says, "and am troubled."

When does he mourn? When is he troubled? He says, "In my
trial." He has in mind the wicked who cause him suffering,
and he calls this suffering his "trial." Do not think that the
evil are in the world for no purpose, and that God makes no
good use of them. Every wicked person lives either that he
may be corrected, or that through him the righteous may be
tried and tested.

Responsory 4 *Tamquam ad latronem*

Have you come out as against a robber,
with swords and clubs to capture me?

Day after day I sat in the temple teaching,
and you did not seize me;
but now, behold, you scourge me,
and lead me away to be crucified.
V.   When they had laid hands on Jesus and were holding
      him, he said:
Day after day I sat in the temple teaching,
and you did not seize me;
but now, behold, you scourge me,
and lead me away to be crucified.

Lesson 5

Would that those who now test us were converted and tried
with us; yet though they continue to try us, let us not hate
them, for we do not know whether any of them will persist
to the end in their evil ways. And most of the time, when you
think you are hating your enemy, you are hating your
brother without knowing it.

Only the devil and his angels are shown to us in the Holy
Scriptures as doomed to eternal fire. It is only their
amendment that is hopeless, and against them we wage a
hidden battle. For this battle the Apostle arms us, saying,
"We are not contending against flesh and blood," that is, not
against human beings whom we see, "but against the
principalities, against the powers, against the rulers of the
darkness of this world." So that you may not think that
demons are the rulers of heaven and earth, he says, "of the
darkness of this world."

He says, "of the world," meaning the lovers of the world—
of the "world," meaning the ungodly and wicked—
the "world" of which the Gospel says, "And the world
knew him not."

Responsory 5   *Tenebrae factae sunt*

Darkness covered the whole land
when Jesus had been crucified;
and about the ninth hour he cried with a loud voice:
My God, my God, why have you forsaken me?
And he bowed his head and handed over his spirit.
V.   Jesus, crying with a loud voice, said:
     Father, into your hands I commend my spirit.
And he bowed his head and handed over his spirit.

Lesson 6

"For I have seen unrighteousness and strife in the city."

See the glory of the cross itself. On the brow of kings that
cross is now placed, the cross which enemies once mocked.
Its power is shown in the result. He has conquered the
world, not by steel, but by wood. The wood of the cross
seemed a fitting object of scorn to his enemies, and standing
before that wood they wagged their heads, saying, "If you
are the Son of God, come down from the cross." He
stretched out his hands to an unbelieving and rebellious
people. If one is just who lives by faith, one who does not
have faith is unrighteous. Therefore when he says
"unrighteousness," understand that it is unbelief. The Lord
then saw unrighteousness and strife in the city, and stretched
out his hands to an unbelieving and rebellious people. And
yet, looking upon them, he said, "Father, forgive them, for
they know not what they do."

Responsory 6   *Ecce quomodo moritur*

See how the righteous one perishes,
and no one takes it to heart.

The righteous are taken away, and no one understands.
From the face of evil the righteous one is taken away,
and his memory shall be in peace.
V. Like a sheep before its shearers is mute, so he opened
    not his mouth.By oppression and judgment he was
    taken away:
And his memory shall be in peace.

When this Responsory is sung rather than recited, repeat all that precedes the
Verse:

See how the righteous . . . in peace.

Third Nocturn

Antiphon 7

God is my helper; it is the Lord who sustains my life.

Psalm 54

Antiphon 8

At Salem is his tabernacle, and his dwelling is in Zion.

Psalm 76

Antiphon 9

I have become like one who has no strength, lost among the
dead.

Psalm 88

V. He has made me dwell in darkness:
R. Like the dead of long ago.

Lesson 7

A Reading from the Letter to the Hebrews.
[4:15—5:10; 9:11-15a]

We do not have a high priest who is unable to sympathize
with our weaknesses, but one who in every respect has been
tempted as we are, yet without sinning. Let us then with
confidence draw near to the throne of grace, that we may
receive mercy and find grace to help in time of need. For
every high priest chosen from among men is appointed to act
on behalf of men in relation to God, to offer gifts and
sacrifices for sins. He can deal gently with the ignorant and
wayward, since he himself is beset with weakness. Because
of this he is bound to offer sacrifice for his own sins as well
as for those of the people.

Responsory 7   *Eram quasi agnus*

I was like a trusting lamb led to the slaughter.
I did not know it was against me
that they devised schemes, saying,
Let us destroy the tree with its fruit;
let us cut him off from the land of the living.
V.   All my enemies whispered together against me,
      and devised evil against me, saying:
Let us destroy the tree with its fruit;
let us cut him off from the land of the living.

Lesson 8

And one does not take the honor upon himself, but he is called by God, just as Aaron was. So also, Christ did not exalt himself to be made a high priest, but was appointed by him who said to him, "You are my Son, this day have I begotten you;" as he says also in another place, "You are a priest for ever after the order of Melchizedek." In the days of his flesh, Jesus offered up prayers and supplications, with loud cries and tears, to him who was able to save him from death, and he was heard for his godly fear. Although he was a Son, he learned obedience through what he suffered; and, being made perfect, he became the source of eternal salvation to all who obey him, being designated by God a high priest after the order of Melchizedek.

Responsory 8 *Velum templi*

The veil of the temple was torn in two,
and the earth shook, and the thief from the cross cried out,
Lord, remember me when you come into your kingdom.
V. The rocks were split, the tombs were opened,
    and many bodies of the saints who slept were raised:
And the earth shook, and the thief from the cross cried out,
Lord, remember me when you come into your kingdom.

Lesson 9

But when Christ appeared as a high priest of the good things that are to come, then, through the greater and more perfect tent (not made with hands, that is, not of this creation), he entered once for all into the Holy Place, taking not the blood of goats and calves but his own blood, thus securing an eternal redemption. For if the sprinkling of defiled persons with the blood of goats and bulls and with the ashes of a heifer sanctifies for the purification of the flesh, how much more shall the blood of Christ, who through the eternal Spirit offered himself without blemish to God, purify your conscience from dead works to serve the living God. Therefore he is the mediator of a new covenant, so that those who are called may receive the promised eternal inheritance.

Responsory 9 *Sepulto Domino*

When the Lord was buried, they sealed the tomb,
rolling a great stone to the door of the tomb;
and they stationed soldiers to guard him.
V. The chief priests gathered before Pilate,
    and petitioned him:
And they stationed soldiers to guard him.

When this Responsory is sung rather than recited, repeat all that precedes the Verse:

When the Lord . . . to guard him.

Lauds

Antiphon 10

God did not spare his own Son, but delivered him up for us all.

Psalm 63,   or   *Psalm 63:1-8*

Antiphon 11

He was led like a lamb to the slaughter, and he opened not his mouth.

Psalm 90, or *Psalm 90:1-12*

Antiphon 12

They shall mourn for him as one mourns for an only child; for the Lord, who is without sin, is slain.

Psalm 143

Antiphon 13

From the gates of hell, O Lord, deliver my soul.

The Song of Hezekiah [Isaiah 38:10-20]

1   In my despair I said,
     "In the noonday of my life I must depart; *
          my unspent years are summoned to the portals of death."

2   And I said,
     "No more shall I see the Lord in the land of the living, *
          never more look on my kind among dwellers on earth.

3   My house is pulled down and I am uncovered, *
          as when a shepherd strikes his tent.

4   My life is rolled up like a bolt of cloth, *
          the threads cut off from the loom.

5   Between sunrise and sunset my life is brought to an end; *
          I cower and hope for the dawn.

6   Like a lion he has crushed all my bones; *
          like a swallow or thrush I utter plaintive cries;
          I mourn like a dove.

7 My weary eyes look up to you; *
    Lord, be my refuge in my affliction."

8 But what can I say? for he has spoken; *
    it is he who has done this.

9 Slow and halting are my steps all my days, *
    because of the bitterness of my spirit.

10 O Lord, I recounted all these things to you
and you rescued me; *
    when entreated, you restored my life.

11 I know now that my bitterness was for my good, *
    for you held me back from the pit of destruction,
    you cast all my sins behind you.

12 The grave does not thank you nor death give you praise; *
    nor do those at the brink of the grave hang on your pror

13 It is the living, O Lord,
    the living who give you thanks as I do this day; *

14 You, Lord, are my Savior; *
    I will praise you with stringed instruments
    all the days of my life, in the house of the Lord.

Ant. From the gates of hell, O Lord, deliver my soul.

Antiphon 14

O Death, I will be your death; O Grave, I will be your destruction.

Psalm 150

1 Praise God in his holy temple; *
    praise him in the firmament of his power.

2   Praise him for his mighty acts; *
      praise him for his excellent greatness.

3   Praise him with the blast of the ram's-horn; *
      praise him with lyre and harp.

4   Praise him with timbrel and dance; *
      praise him with strings and pipe.

5   Praise him with resounding cymbals; *
      praise him with loud-clanging cymbals.

6   Let everything that has breath *
      praise the LORD.

Ant.   O Death, I will be your death;
       O Grave, I will be your destruction.

V.   My flesh also shall rest in hope:
R.   You will not let your holy One see corruption.

All stand. During the singing of the following Canticle, the candles at the Altar, and all other lights in the church (except the one remaining at the top of the triangular candlestick), are extinguished.

Antiphon

Now the women sitting at the tomb made lamentation, weeping for the Lord.

Canticle 16:   Benedictus Dominus Deus Israel

After the Canticle, during the repetition of the Antiphon, the remaining candle is taken from the stand and hidden beneath or behind the Altar, or in some other convenient place.

All kneel for the singing of the following anthem

Christus factus est

Christ for us became obedient unto death, even death on a cross; therefore God has highly exalted him and bestowed on him the Name which is above every name.

A brief silence is observed.

The following Psalm is then said quietly. If it is sung, it is customary to monotone alternate verses.

Psalm 51

The Officiant says the Collect without chant, and without the usual conclusion.

Almighty God, we pray you graciously to behold this your family, for whom our Lord Jesus Christ was willing to be betrayed, and given into the hands of sinners, and to suffer death upon the cross.

Nothing further is said; but a noise is made, and the remaining candle is brought from its hiding place and replaced on the stand.

By its light the ministers and people depart in silence.

Additional Directions

This book provides for the full ancient form of the service: Matins, subdivided into three Nocturns, and Lauds. If desired, the service may be shortened somewhat by using the shorter form indicated for certain of the Psalms. The first two responsories of each Nocturn may also be omitted.

In preparation for the service, a large triangular candlestick with fifteen candles is placed at the liturgical south side of the sanctuary. One candle is extinguished at the end of each Psalm, and at the end of the Song of Hezekiah. Finally, during the singing of the canticle Benedictus, the candles at the Altar, and all other lights (except the one at the top of the triangular stand), are extinguished.

There should be no musical prelude or postlude at this service, nor should a processional cross or torches be carried, or hymns sung, or sermons preached.

The ministers, servers, and choir vest in the manner customary for choir offices. The officiant may wear a tippet over the surplice.

The appointed antiphons are sung or recited in full before and after each Psalm. The Psalms themselves are sung or recited antiphonally. Gloria Patri is not used at this service.

Each group of lessons is announced only at the beginning, as indicated in the text. The usual concluding formula is omitted.

The successive letters of the Hebrew alphabet, prefixed to the verses of the readings from Lamentations, are an integral part of the traditional chant, and should not be omitted when these lessons are sung. (In the Hebrew original, each verse begins with the letter indicated.)

If the responsories after the lessons are recited rather than sung, the congregation reads the parts in italics. In musical settings the responsories may be sung in full by the choir or by all; the verse [V.] may be sung by a solo voice. The repetition of the first part of the text in Responsories 3, 6, and 9 is intended for use in musical settings only.

If a much shorter form of the service is desired, Nocturns 2 and 3 and the second or third Psalm of Lauds (Psalm 90 or 143) may be omitted. In this case two candles are extinguished after each Psalm. Alternatively, Nocturns 2 and 3 and two of the Lauds' Psalms may be omitted, and a seven-branched candlestick used.

On Maundy Thursday

At the Foot-Washing

If it is desired to introduce the ceremony of foot-washing by a brief address, the following may be used.

Fellow servants of our Lord Jesus Christ: On the night before his death, Jesus set an example for his disciples by washing their feet, an act of humble service. He taught that strength and growth in the life of the Kingdom of God come not by power, authority, or even miracle, but by such lowly service. We all need to remember his example, but none stand more in need of this reminder than those whom the Lord has called to the ordained ministry.

Therefore, I invite you [who have been appointed as representatives of the congregation and] who share in the royal priesthood of Christ, to come forward, that I may recall whose servant I am by following the example of my Master. But come remembering his admonition that what will be done for you is also to be done by you to others, for "a servant is not greater than his master, nor is one who is sent greater than the one who sent him. If you know these things, blessed are you if you do them."

On Reserving the Sacrament

When the Sacrament is to be reserved for administration on Good Friday, it should be kept in a separate chapel or other place apart from the main sanctuary of the church, in order that on Good Friday the attention of the congregation may be on the bare main Altar.

On the Stripping of the Altar

If the custom of stripping the Altar is observed as a public ceremony, it takes place after the Maundy Thursday liturgy. It may be done in silence; or it may be accompanied by the recitation of Psalm 22, which is said without Gloria Patri. The following antiphon may be said before and after the Psalm.

They divide my garments among them; they cast lots for my clothing.

Agapé for Maundy Thursday

The celebration of festal meals is not appropriate during Holy Week. In Christian tradition such festivities take place only after the Lenten fast has been completed by the celebration of the Great Vigil — which is the Passover Feast of Christians — and the reception of Easter Communion.

If it is desired to share a meal after the Maundy Thursday Eucharist, the following order may be observed.

A meatless meal is to be preferred. The setting should be austere and the foods sparse and simple. Appropriate foods include soup, cheese, olives, dried fruit, bread, and wine. It is suitable that the bread and wine for the meal be brought to the Altar at the time of the Offertory (along with special offerings for the hungry), and after the service taken to the room where the meal is to take place.

The following blessings are recited by the Celebrant at the beginning of the meal, all standing.

Over Wine

Blessed are you, O Lord our God, King of the universe. You create the fruit of the vine; and on this night you have refreshed us with the cup of salvation in the Blood of your Son Jesus Christ. Glory to you for ever and ever. *Amen.*

Over Bread

Blessed are you, O Lord our God, King of the universe. You
bring forth bread from the earth; and on this night you have
given us the bread of life in the Body of your Son Jesus
Christ. As grain scattered upon the earth is gathered into one
loaf, so gather your Church in every place into the kingdom
of your Son. To you be glory and power for ever and ever.
Amen.

Over the Other Foods

Blessed are you, O Lord our God, King of the universe. You
have blessed the earth to bring forth food to satisfy our
hunger. Let this food strengthen us in the fast that is before
us, that following our Savior in the way of the cross, we may
come to the joy of his resurrection. For yours is the kingdom
and the power and the glory, now and for ever. *Amen.*

*During the meal or toward its close, a person appointed reads the
seventeenth chapter of the Gospel according to John.*

*The agapé concludes with a psalm, such as Psalm 69:1-23, or with a
song, or with a prayer, or with a blessing or dismissal.*

*If an agapé is held, the ceremony of stripping the Altar is deferred until
after the meal.*

*The form for the agapé given above may also be used in private homes
on this night.*

Blessings Over Food at Easter

These blessings are appropriate for use by households at the principal meal on Easter Day. They may be used at a parish meal following the Easter Vigil. They may also be used over foods brought to the church for blessing.

Over Wine

Blessed are you, O Lord our God, creator of the fruit of the vine: Grant that we who share this wine, which gladdens our hearts, may share for ever the new life of the true Vine, your Son Jesus Christ our Lord. *Amen.*

Over Bread

Blessed are you, O Lord our God; you bring forth bread from the earth and make the risen Lord to be for us the Bread of life: Grant that we who daily seek the bread which sustains our bodies may also hunger for the food of everlasting life, Jesus Christ our Lord. *Amen.*

Over Lamb

Stir up our memory, O Lord, as we eat this Easter lamb that, remembering Israel of old, who in obedience to your command ate the Paschal lamb and was delivered from the bondage of slavery, we, your new Israel, may rejoice in the resurrection of Jesus Christ, the true Lamb who has delivered us from the bondage of sin and death, and who lives and reigns for ever and ever. *Amen.*

Over Eggs

O Lord our God, in celebration of the Paschal feast we have prepared these eggs from your creation: Grant that they may be to us a sign of the new life and immortality promised to those who follow your Son, Jesus Christ our Lord. *Amen.*

Over Other Foods

Blessed are you, O Lord our God; you have given us the risen Savior to be the Shepherd of your people: Lead us, by him, to springs of living waters, and feed us with the food that endures to eternal life; where with you, O Father, and with the Holy Spirit, he lives and reigns, one God, for ever and ever. *Amen.*

Blessing in Homes at Easter

*Where it is customary to invite the parish priest to the homes of
parishioners during the Fifty Days of Easter, this blessing may be used.*

The Celebrant begins with the following or some other greeting.

Peace be to this house, and to all who dwell in it.

Psalm 114 is then sung or said with one of the following antiphons:

Alleluia. The Lord is risen indeed: Come let us adore him.
Alleluia.

or this

I saw water proceeding out of the temple; from the right side
it flowed, alleluia; and all those to whom that water came
shall be saved, and shall say, alleluia, alleluia.

When Israel came out of Egypt, *
    the house of Jacob from a people of strange speech,
Judah became God's sanctuary *
    and Israel his dominion.
The sea beheld it and fled; *
    Jordan turned and went back.
The mountains skipped like rams, *
    and the little hills like young sheep.

What ailed you, O sea, that you fled? *
   O Jordan, that you turned back?
You mountains, that you skipped like rams? *
   you little hills like young sheep?
Tremble, O earth, at the presence of the Lord, *
   at the presence of the God of Jacob,
Who turned the hard rock into a pool of water *
   and flint-stone into a flowing spring.
Glory to the Father, and to the Son, and to the Holy Spirit: *
   as it was in the beginning, is now, and will be for ever. Amen.

The antiphon is then repeated.

Another psalm, such as Psalm 118, may be used in place of Psalm 114, or a canticle may be substituted. Suitable canticles are Christ our Passover, the Song of Moses, and the Song to the Lamb.

Celebrant	The Lord be with you.
People	And also with you.
Celebrant	Let us pray.

The Celebrant says one of the following Collects, or some other Collect of the Easter Season.

Grant, we pray, Almighty God, that we who celebrate with awe the Paschal feast may be found worthy to attain to everlasting joys; through Jesus Christ our Lord, who lives and reigns with you and the Holy Spirit, one God, now and for ever. *Amen.*

or this

Almighty and everlasting God, who in the Paschal mystery established the new covenant of reconciliation: Grant that all who have been reborn into the fellowship of Christ's Body may show forth in their lives what they profess by their faith; through Jesus Christ our Lord, who lives and reigns with you and the Holy Spirit, one God, for ever and ever. *Amen.*

The Celebrant then says this prayer

Visit, O blessed Lord, this home with the gladness of your presence. Bless *all* who *live* here with the gift of your love; and grant that *they* may manifest your love [to each other and] to all whose lives *they* touch. May *they* grow in grace and in the knowledge and love of you; guide, comfort, and strengthen *them*; and preserve *them* in peace, O Jesus Christ, now and for ever. *Amen.*

The Celebrant may say one of the two following blessings:

May God the Father, who by Baptism adopts us as his children, grant you grace. *Amen.*

May God the Son, who sanctified a home at Nazareth, fill you with love. *Amen.*

May God the Holy Spirit, who has made the Church one family, keep you in peace. *Amen.*

or this

May Almighty God, who has redeemed us and made us his children through the resurrection of his Son our Lord, bestow upon you the riches of his blessing. *Amen.*

May God, who through the water of baptism has raised us from sin into newness of life, make you holy and worthy to be united with Christ for ever. *Amen.*

May God, who has brought us out of bondage to sin into true and lasting freedom in the Redeemer, bring you to your eternal inheritance. *Amen.*

And the blessing of God Almighty, the Father, the Son, and the Holy Spirit, be upon you and remain with you for ever. *Amen.*

The Peace may then be exchanged.

Rogation Procession

The Rogation Days are traditionally observed on the Monday, Tuesday, and Wednesday before Ascension Day. They may, however, be observed on other days, depending on local conditions and the convenience of the congregation.

Anciently, the observance consisted of an outdoor procession which culminated in a special celebration of the Eucharist. In more recent centuries, the procession has frequently taken place on a Sunday afternoon, apart from the Eucharist.

If the Rogation Procession is held on a Sunday or Principal Feast, it should take place apart from or following the Proper Eucharist of the Day. Under these conditions the procession concludes with a suitable prayer and a blessing.

Hymns, psalms, canticles, and anthems are sung during the procession. The following are appropriate:

Canticle 1 or 12 (Benedicite)
Psalm 103 (Refrain: "Bless the Lord, O my soul")
Psalm 104 (Refrain: "Hallelujah").

At suitable places the procession may halt for appropriate Bible readings and prayers.

In addition to the readings listed on page 930 of the Prayer Book, any of the following passages are appropriate:

Genesis 8:13-23	Ezekiel 34:25-31
Leviticus 26:1-13(14-20)	James 4:7-11
Deuteronomy 8:1-10(11-20)	Matthew 6:25-34
Hosea 2:18-23	John 12:23-26

Suitable prayers include the following:Prayers 1, 29, 34, 38, 40-44, and Thanksgivings 1, 8, 9 from the section "Prayers and Thanksgivings" in the Prayer Book. Also, the following

Almighty and everlasting God, Creator of all things and giver of all life, let your blessing be upon this (seed, livestock, plough, forest, _____) and grant that *it* may serve to your glory and the welfare of your people; through Jesus Christ our Lord. *Amen.*

Customarily, the Great Litany is begun as the procession enters the church. The following petitions may be inserted following the third petition on page 151 of the Prayer Book:

That it may please thee to grant favorable weather, temperate rain, and fruitful seasons, that there may be food and drink for all thy creatures,
We beseech thee to hear us, good Lord.

That it may please thee to bless the lands and waters, and all who work upon them to bring forth food and all things needful for thy people,
We beseech thee to hear us, good Lord.

That it may please thee to look with favor upon all who care for the earth, the water, and the air, that the riches of thy creation may abound from age to age,
We beseech thee to hear us, good Lord.

At the conclusion of the Litany, after the Kyries, the Eucharist begins with the Salutation and one of the Proper Collects for Rogation Days.

If the procession cannot take place out of doors, the service may begin with the Great Litany, which may be sung in procession in the church.

If the Liturgy does not begin with the Great Litany, it is suggested that Form V be used for the Prayers of the People, and that the following petitions be added after the eighth petition on page 390:

For favorable weather, temperate rains, and fruitful seasons, that there may be food and drink for all your creatures, we pray to you, O Lord.

For your blessing upon the lands and waters, and all who work upon them to bring forth food and all things needful for your people, we pray to you, O Lord.

For all who care for the earth, the water, and the air, that the riches of your creation may abound from age to age, we pray to you, O Lord.

Vigil for the Eve of All Saints' Day

or the Sunday after All Saints' Day

When a Baptismal Vigil of All Saints is observed, it begins with the Service of Light, page 109 of the Prayer Book (substituting, if desired, the Gloria in excelsis for the Phos hilaron), and continues with the Salutation and Collect of the Day. Three or more Lessons are read before the Gospel, each followed by a period of silence and a Psalm, Canticle, or hymn. Holy Baptism or Confirmation (beginning with the Presentation of the Candidates), or the Renewal of Baptismal Vows, Prayer Book page 292, follows the Sermon.

The Call of Abraham
Genesis 12:1-8

Psalm 113

Daniel Delivered from the Lions' Den
Daniel 6:(1-15)16-23

Canticle 2 *or* 13

The Testament and Death of Mattathias
1 Maccabees 2:49-64

Psalm 1

The Martyrdom of the Seven Brothers
2 Maccabees 6:1-2; 7:1-23

Psalm 111

The Eulogy of the Ancestors *
Ecclesiasticus 44:1-10,13-14

Psalm 116

Surrounded by a Great Cloud of Witnesses †
Hebrews 11:32(33-38)39—12:2

Psalm 149 *

The Reward of the Saints *
Revelation 7:2-4,9-17

The Beatitudes *
Matthew 5:1-12

or **"I will give you rest"**
  Matthew 11:27-30

or **The Resurrection and the Great Commission** °
  Matthew 28:1-10,16-20

* Proper Readings and Psalm for the Eucharist of All Saints.
† Appointed also for Morning Prayer on All Saints' Day.
° On Saturday evening only.

Service for All Hallows' Eve

This service may be used on the evening of October 31, known as All Hallows' Eve. Suitable festivities and entertainments may take place before or after this service, and a visit may be made to a cemetery or burial place.

The rite begins with the Service of Light, page 109 of the Prayer Book, using the Prayer for Light appointed for Festivals of Saints.

After the Phos hilaron, two or more of the following lessons are read, each followed by a Psalm, Canticle, or hymn, and a Prayer.

The Witch of Endor
1 Samuel 28:3-25
(It is appropriate that this lesson be read by a narrator, and by other readers for Saul, the witch, and Samuel.)

Psalm 130

Let us pray. *(Silence)*

Almighty and everliving God, you have made all things in your wisdom and established the boundaries of life and death: Grant that we may obey your voice in this world, and in the world to come may enjoy that rest and peace which you have appointed for your people; through Jesus Christ who is Resurrection and Life, and who lives and reigns for ever and ever. *Amen.*

The Vision of Eliphaz the Temanite
Job 4:12-21

Psalm 13, *or* Psalm 108:1-6

Let us pray. *(Silence)*

You, O Lord, have made us from the dust of the earth and to dust our bodies shall return; yet you have also breathed your Spirit upon us and called us to new life in you: Have mercy upon us, now and at the hour of our death; through Jesus Christ, our mediator and advocate. *Amen.*

The Valley of Dry Bones
Ezekiel 37:1-14

Psalm 143:1-11

Let us pray. *(Silence)*

O God, you have called your people to your service from age to age. Do not give us over to death, but raise us up to serve you, to praise you, and to glorify your holy Name; through Jesus Christ our Lord. *Amen.*

The War in Heaven
Revelation 12:(1-6)7-12

Psalm 103:17-22, *or* Canticle 1 (parts I & IV) *or* Canticle 12 (Invocation, Part III, Doxology)

Let us pray. *(Silence)*

O most merciful and mighty God, your son Jesus Christ was born of the Blessed Virgin Mary to bring us salvation and to establish your kingdom on earth: Grant that Michael and all your angels may defend your people against Satan and every evil foe, and that at the last we may come to that heavenly country where your saints for ever sing your praise; through Jesus Christ our Lord. *Amen.*

A homily, sermon, or instruction may follow the Readings.

The service then concludes with the singing of Te Deum laudamus or some other song of praise, the Lord's Prayer, the Collect of All Saints' Day, and a blessing or dismissal.

Pastoral Services

Welcoming New People
To a Congregation

If it is desired to welcome new people to the congregation publicly, it is suitable that they be introduced in the following manner.

Immediately before the Peace, the persons are asked to come forward, and are introduced briefly, preferably by a member of the congregation.

The celebrant then begins the exchange of the Peace, in the course of which those who have been introduced are greeted personally by the celebrant and members of the congregation as convenient.

When Members
Leave a Congregation

When persons leave a congregation, it is suitable that, on their last Sunday, the fact be mentioned before the Prayers of the People, and that they be prayed for by name in those Prayers.

They are greeted personally by the celebrant and lay officials of the congregation at the time of the Peace, or at the end of the service.

Concerning the Catechumenate

The catechumenate is a period of training and instruction in Christian understandings about God, human relationships, and the meaning of life, which culminates in the reception of the Sacraments of Christian Initiation.

The systematic instruction and formation of its catechumens is a solemn responsibility of the Christian community. Traditionally, the preparation of catechumens is a responsibility of the bishop, which is shared with the presbyters, deacons, and appointed lay catechists of the diocese.

Principles of Implementation

1. A catechumen is defined as an unbaptized adult. These rites are appropriate for use only with such persons.

2. During the period of the catechumenate, the context of catechesis is a continual reflection on Scripture, Christian prayer, worship, and the catechumen's gifts for ministry and work for justice and peace. These elements are more or less a part of each catechetical session.

3. The principal curriculum for each catechetical session is reflection on the respective readings of the Sunday Eucharistic Lectionary as these illumine the faith journey of catechumens, sponsors, and catechists.

4. The catechetical methodology of the catechumenal and baptismal rites is: experience first, then reflect. As the catechumen journeys from inquiry to baptism, there is formation of an ability to discern God's activity in the events of one's life. It is recommended that the services not be discussed prior to their celebration. It is appropriate that sponsors be well prepared for their ministry in the respective services and to guide and support their catechumen during the celebration.

5. The catechumenate exists throughout the year in the parish, and persons may enter at any time. The catechumenate is of undetermined length for each catechumen. The appropriate time for the call to Candidacy for Baptism is discerned by sponsors, catechists, and clergy on behalf of the local congregation. Baptism of catechumens is normally reserved for the Great Vigil of Easter.

6. Since the catechumenate is ecclesial formation for the ministry of the baptized, it is appropriate that the catechists be representative of the diversity of the local congregation.

7. It is appropriate for those catechumens baptized at the Great Vigil of Easter to join the ministry of sponsor or catechist for new catechumens at the conclusion of the Great Fifty Days.

The Catechumenate is marked by three stages.

Stage 1. The Pre-catechumenal Period. To this stage belong inquirers' classes with sufficient preparation to enable persons to determine that they wish to become Christians. It is a time during which those who have been initially attracted to the Christian community are guided to examine and test their motives, in order that they may freely commit themselves to pursue a disciplined exploration of the implications of Christian living.

Stage 2. The Catechumenate. Entry into the catechumenate is by a public liturgical act (which may take place for individuals or groups at any time) at the principal Sunday liturgy. Normatively, the act includes signing with the cross. To this stage belong regular association with the worshiping community, the practice of life in accordance with the Gospel (including service to the poor and neglected), encouragement and instruction in thelife of prayer, and basic instruction in the history of salvation as revealed in the Holy Scriptures of the Old and New Testaments. This stage will vary in length according to the needs of the individual. For those persons who, although unbaptized, already possess an understanding and appreciation of the Christian religion, it might be relatively short.

Each person to be admitted a catechumen is presented by a sponsor who normally accompanies the catechumen through the process of candidacy and serves as sponsor at Holy Baptism.

Admission to the catechumenate is an appropriate time to determine the name by which one desires to be known in the Christian community. This may be one's given name, a new name legally changed, or an additional name of Christian significance.

From the time of admission, a catechumen is regarded as a part of the

Christian community. For example, a person who dies during the catechumenate receives a Christian burial.

Stage 3. Candidacy for Baptism. To this stage belong a series of liturgical acts leading up to baptism. These ordinarily take place on a series of Sundays preceding one of the stated days for baptism, and involve public prayer for the candidates, who are present at the services as a group, accompanied by their sponsors. When the Sacrament of Holy Baptism is administered at Easter, enrollment as a candidate normally takes place at the beginning of Lent; when baptisms are planned for the Feast of the Baptism of Our Lord, the enrollment takes place at the beginning of Advent.

In addition to these public acts, this stage involves the private disciplines of fasting, examination of conscience, and prayer, in order that the candidates will be spiritually and emotionally ready for baptism. It is appropriate that, in accordance with ancient custom, the sponsors support their candidates by joining them in prayer and fasting.

A fourth period immediately follows the administration of Holy Baptism. In the case of persons baptized at the Great Vigil, it extends over the Fifty Days of Easter. This period is devoted to such activities, formal and informal, as will assist the newly baptized to experience the fullness of the corporate life of the Church and to gain a deeper understanding of the meaning of the Sacraments.

The bishop, the bishop's representative, or the rector (or priest-in-charge) of the congregation should preside at the rites of Admission and Enrollment.

It should be noted that the rites and prayers which follow are appropriate for use only with persons preparing for baptism. Validly baptized Christians present at instruction classes to deepen their understanding of the faith, including members of other Christian bodies preparing to be received into the Episcopal Church, are under no circumstances to be considered catechumens. The same is true of persons preparing to re-affirm their baptismal vows after having abandoned the practice of the Christian religion, since "The bond which God establishes in Baptism is indissoluble" (Prayer Book, page 298).

Preparation of Adults for Holy Baptism: The Catechumenate

Admission of Catechumens

The admission of catechumens may take place at any time of the year, within a principal Sunday liturgy.

After the sermon (or after the Creed) the Celebrant invites those to be admitted as catechumens to come forward with their sponsors.

The Celebrant then asks the following question of those to be admitted. If desired, the question may be asked of each person individually.

What do you seek?

Answer Life in Christ.

The Celebrant then says,

Jesus said, "The first commandment is this: Hear, O Israel: The Lord our God is the only Lord. Love the Lord your God with all your heart, with all your soul, and with all your strength. The second is this: Love your neighbor as yourself. There is no other commandment greater than these." Do you accept these commandments?

Answer I do.

| *Celebrant* | Do you promise to be regular in attending the worship of God and in receiving instruction? |
| *Answer* | I do. |

| *Celebrant* | Will you open your ears to hear the Word of God and your heart and mind to receive the Lord Jesus? |
| *Answer* | I will, with God's help. |

The Celebrant then addresses the sponsors

Will you who sponsor *these persons* support *them* by prayer and example and help *them* to grow in the knowledge and love of God?

| *Sponsors* | I will. |

Those to be admitted kneel. The sponsors remain standing, and place a hand upon the shoulder of the one they are sponsoring, while the Celebrant extends a hand toward them and says

May Almighty God, our heavenly Father, who has put the desire into your *hearts* to seek the grace of our Lord Jesus Christ, grant you the power of the Holy Spirit to persevere in this intention and to grow in faith and understanding.

| *People* | Amen. |

Each of those to be admitted is presented by name to the Celebrant, who, with the thumb, marks a cross on the forehead of each, saying

N., receive the sign of the Cross on your forehead and in your heart, in the Name of the Father, and of the Son, and of the Holy Spirit.

| *People* | Amen. |

The Sponsors also mark a cross on the foreheads of their catechumens.

The catechumens and sponsors then return to their places.

The Liturgy continues with (the Creed and) the Prayers of the People, in the course of which prayer is offered for the new catechumens by name.

If any of the catechumens, after consultation with the celebrant, wishes to renounce a former way of worship, an appropriately worded renunciation may be included immediately following the first question and answer.

During the Catechumenate

During this period, and continuing through the period of Candidacy, formal instruction is given to the catechumens. At the conclusion of each session, a period of silence is observed, during which the catechumens pray for themselves and one another. Sponsors and other baptized persons present offer their prayers for the catechumens. The instructor then says one or two of the following or some other suitable prayers, and concludes by laying a hand individually on the head of each catechumen in silence. It is traditional that this act be performed by the instructor, whether bishop, priest, deacon, or lay catechist.

1

O God, the creator and savior of all flesh, look with mercy on your *children* whom you call to yourself in love. Cleanse *their hearts* and guard *them* as *they prepare* to receive your Sacraments that, led by your Holy Spirit, *they* may be united with your Son, and enter into the inheritance of your sons and daughters; through Jesus Christ our Lord. *Amen.*

2

O God of truth, of beauty, and of goodness, we give you
thanks that from the beginning of creation you have revealed
yourself in the things that you have made; and that in every
nation, culture, and language there have been those who,
seeing your works, have worshiped you and sought to do
your will. Accept our prayers for *these* your *servants* whom
you have called to know and love you as you have been
perfectly revealed in your Son Jesus Christ our Redeemer, and
bring *them* with joy to new birth in the waters of Baptism;
through Jesus Christ our Lord. *Amen.*

3

O God of righteousness and truth, you inaugurated your
victory over the forces of deceit and sin by the Advent of
your Son: Give to *these catechumens* a growing
understanding of the truth as it is in Jesus; and grant that
they, being cleansed from sin and born again in the waters of
Baptism, may glorify with us the greatness of your Name;
through Jesus Christ our Lord. *Amen.*

4

O God, in your pity you looked upon a fallen world, and
sent your only Son among us to vanquish the powers of
wickedness. Deliver *these* your *servants* from slavery to sin
and evil. Purify *their* desires and thoughts with the light of
your Holy Spirit. Nourish *them* with your holy Word,
strengthen *them* in faith, and confirm *them* in good works;
through Jesus Christ our Lord. *Amen.*

5

Look down in mercy, Lord, upon *these catechumens* now
being taught in your holy Word. Open *their* ears to hear and

their hearts to obey. Bring to *their minds their* past sins,
committed against you and against *their* neighbors, that *they*
may truly repent of them. And in your mercy preserve *them*
in *their* resolve to seek your kingdom and your
righteousness; through Jesus Christ our Lord. *Amen.*

6

Drive out of *these catechumens*, Lord God, every trace of
wickedness. Protect *them* from the Evil One. Bring *them* to
the saving waters of baptism, and make *them* yours for ever;
through Jesus Christ our Lord. *Amen.*

7

Lord Jesus Christ, loving Redeemer of all, you alone have
the power to save. At your Name every knee shall bow,
whether in heaven, on earth, or under the earth. We pray to
you for *these catechumens* who *seek* to serve you, the one
true God. Send your light into *their hearts*, protect *them*
from the hatred of the Evil One, heal in *them* the wounds of
sin, and strengthen *them* against temptation. Give *them* a
love of your commandments, and courage to live always by
your Gospel, and so prepare *them* to receive your Spirit; you
who live and reign for ever and ever. *Amen.*

8

Most merciful God, behold and sustain *these catechumens*
who *seek* to know you more fully: Free *them* from the grasp
of Satan, and make *them* bold to renounce all sinful desires
that entice *them* from loving you; that, coming in faith to
the Sacrament of Baptism, *they* may commit *themselves* to
you, receive the seal of the Holy Spirit, and share with us in
the eternal priesthood of Jesus Christ our Lord. *Amen.*

9

Lord God, unfailing light and source of light, by the death and resurrection of your Christ you have cast out hatred and deceit, and poured upon the human family the light of truth and love: Look upon *these catechumens* whom you have called to enter your covenant, free *them* from the power of the Prince of darkness, and number *them* among the children of promise; through Jesus Christ our Lord. *Amen.*

10

Stir up, O Lord, the *wills* of *these catechumens*, and assist *them* by your grace, that *they* may bring forth plenteously the fruit of good works, and receive from you a rich reward; through Jesus Christ our Lord. *Amen.*

Enrollment of Candidates for Baptism

The enrollment of candidates for Baptism at the Great Vigil of Easter normally takes place on the First Sunday in Lent. For those preparing for Baptism on the Feast of our Lord's Baptism, it takes place on the First Sunday of Advent.

The large book in which the names of the candidates for Baptism are to be written is placed where it can easily be seen and used.

After the Creed, the catechumens to be enrolled are invited to come forward with their sponsors.

A Catechist, or other lay representative of the congregation, presents them to the bishop or priest with the following or similar words

I present to you *these catechumens* who *have* been
strengthened by God's grace and supported by the example
and prayers of this congregation, and I ask that *they* be
enrolled as *candidates* for Holy Baptism.

The Celebrant asks the sponsors

Have they been regular in attending the worship of God and
in receiving instruction?

Sponsors   They have. (*He* has.)

Celebrant   *Are they* seeking by prayer, study, and example to
          pattern their lives in accordance with the Gospel?

Sponsors   They are. (*He* is.)

The Celebrant asks the sponsors and congregation

As God is your witness, do you approve the enrolling of
these catechumens as *candidates* for Holy Baptism?

Answer   We do.

The Celebrant addresses the catechumens

Do you desire to be baptized?

Catechumens   I do.

The Celebrant then says

In the Name of God, and with the consent of this
congregation, I accept you as *candidates* for Holy Baptism,
and direct that your *names* be written in this book. God
grant that *they* may also be written in the Book of Life.

*The candidates then publicly write their names in the book; or, if
necessary, someone else may write the names. Each name is said aloud at
the time of writing. The sponsors may also sign the book.*

The candidates remain together at the front of the church while the Deacon, or other person appointed, leads the following litany:

In peace let us pray to the Lord, saying "Lord, have mercy."

For *these catechumens*, that *they* may remember this day on which *they were* chosen, and remain for ever grateful for this heavenly blessing, let us pray to the Lord.
Lord, have mercy.

That *they* may use this Lenten season wisely, joining with us in acts of self-denial and in performing works of mercy, let us pray to the Lord.
Lord, have mercy.

For *their* teachers, that they may make known to those whom they teach the riches of the Word of God, let us pray to the Lord.
Lord, have mercy.

For *their* sponsor(s), that in *their* private *lives* and public actions *they* may show to *these candidates* a pattern of life in accordance with the Gospel, let us pray to the Lord.
Lord, have mercy.

For *their families* and friends, that they may place no obstacles in the way of *these candidates*, but rather assist *them* to follow the promptings of the Spirit, let us pray to the Lord.
Lord, have mercy.

For this congregation, that [during this Lenten season] it may abound in love and persevere in prayer, let us pray to the Lord.
Lord, have mercy.

For our Bishop, and for all the clergy and people, let us pray to the Lord.
Lord, have mercy.

For our President, for the leaders of the nations, and for all in authority, let us pray to the Lord.
Lord, have mercy.

For the sick and the sorrowful, and for those in any need or trouble, let us pray to the Lord.
Lord, have mercy.

For _____, let us pray to the Lord.
Lord, have mercy.

For all who have died in the hope of the resurrection, and for all the departed, let us pray to the Lord.
Lord, have mercy.

In the communion of [_____ and of all the] saints, let us commend ourselves, and one another, and all our life, to Christ our God.
To you, O Lord our God.

Silence

The Celebrant says the following prayer with hands extended over the candidates

Immortal God, Lord Jesus Christ, the protector of all who come to you, the life of those who believe, and the resurrection of the dead: We call upon you for *these* your *servants* who *desire* the grace of spiritual rebirth in the Sacrament of Holy Baptism. Accept *them*, Lord Christ, as you promised when you said, "Ask, and it will be given you; seek, and you will find; knock, and it will be opened to you." Give now, we pray, to those who ask, let those who seek find, open the gate to those who knock; that *these* your *servants* may receive the everlasting benediction of your heavenly washing, and come to that promised kingdom which you have prepared, and where you live and reign for ever and ever. *Amen.*

The candidates then return to their places and the Liturgy continues with the Confession of Sin or with the Peace.

During Candidacy

On the Sundays preceding their baptism, the candidates attend public worship with their sponsors, and both the candidates and sponsors are prayed for by name in the Prayers of the People. (When Eucharistic Prayer D is used, however, it is appropriate that the names be inserted at the place provided in that prayer.)

In addition, the following prayers and blessings may be used immediately before the Prayers of the People, especially on the Third, Fourth, and Fifth Sundays in Lent (or, the Second, Third, and Fourth Sundays of Advent). When these prayers are used, the candidates and sponsors are called forward. The candidates kneel or bow their heads. The sponsors each place a hand upon the shoulder of their candidate.

The Celebrant then calls the people to prayer in these or similar words

Let us pray in silence, dearly beloved, for *these candidates* who *are* preparing to receive the illumination of the Holy Spirit in the Sacrament of Baptism.

All pray in silence.

The Celebrant says one of the following prayers:

Lord God, in the beginning of creation you called forth light to dispel the darkness that lay upon the face of the deep: Deliver *these* your *servants* from the powers of evil and illumine *them* with the light of your presence, that with open eyes and glad *hearts they* may worship you and serve you, now and for ever; through Jesus Christ our Lord. *Amen.*

or this

Lord Christ, true Light who enlightens every one: Shine, we
pray, in the *hearts* of *these candidates*, that *they* may
clearly see the way that leads to life eternal, and may follow
it without stumbling; for you yourself are the Way, O Christ,
as you are the Truth and the Life; and you live and reign for
ever and ever. *Amen.*

or this

Come, O Holy Spirit, come; come as the wind and cleanse;
come as the fire and burn; convict, convert, and consecrate
the *minds* and *hearts* of *these* your *servants,* to *their* great
good and to your great glory; who with the Father and the
Son are one God, now and for ever. *Amen.*

The Celebrant lays a hand on the head of each candidate in silence.

The Celebrant then adds one of the following blessings:

May Almighty God bestow upon you the blessing of his
mercy, and give you an understanding of the wisdom that
leads to salvation; through Christ our Lord. *Amen.*

or this

May Almighty God keep your steps from wandering from
the way of truth, and cause you to walk in the paths of peace
and love; through Christ our Lord. *Amen.*

or this

May Almighty God nourish you with true knowledge of the
catholic faith, and grant you to persevere in every good
work; through Christ our Lord. *Amen.*

*The candidates and sponsors return to their places and the Liturgy
continues.*

Additional Directions

1. When there are catechumens who are candidates for baptism at the Great Vigil of Easter, it is appropriate in any year with the consent of the Bishop to use the Sunday lectionary for Year A during Lent and the Great Fifty Days of Easter.

2. In parishes where catechumens are dismissed from the Sunday Eucharist, it is appropriate that this take place following the sermon. The celebrant should send them forth from the Assembly with a blessing and commission to study the Word they have received. Catechumens should be accompanied from the Assembly by their sponsors and catechists to the place for the catechetical session.

3. It is appropriate that the Apostles' (or Nicene) Creed be given to the Candidates for Baptism on the Third Sunday in Lent and the Lord's Prayer be given to them on the Fifth Sunday in Lent. (This may follow the Prayers for the candidates for Baptism on those Sundays. See page 126.)

The Presentation of the Creed (Third Sunday in Lent)

Either the Apostles' or Nicene Creed may be given to the Candidates, but preference is here indicated for the Apostles' Creed. On the occasion of their Baptism at the Great Vigil of Easter, candidates will recite the Apostles' Creed in the Baptismal Covenant.

Immediately after the Sermon, candidates and sponsors are called forward for (the Prayers for the Candidates for Baptism, and for) the Presentation of the Creed. The Candidates kneel or bow their heads. The sponsors each place a hand upon the shoulder of their candidate.

One of the catechists says

Let the candidate(s) for Baptism now receive the Creed from the Church.

The People and Celebrant say the Creed, all standing.

Apostles' Creed—BCP, page 66 or 96
(or Nicene Creed—BCP, page 326 or 358)

The Celebrant concludes (dismissal of the candidates is optional)

(Candidate(s) go in peace.) May the Lord remain with you always. *Amen.*

Candidates and sponsors are dismissed, or return to their places in the congregation.

The Presentation of the Lord's Prayer (Fifth Sunday in Lent)

When the candidates have been baptized at the Great Vigil of Easter and take part in their first celebration of the Eucharist, they will join the rest of the faithful in saying the Lord's Prayer.

Immediately after the Sermon, candidates and sponsors are called forward for (the Prayers for the Candidates for Baptism and for) the Presentation of the Lord's Prayer. (The Creed may be omitted on this day.) The candidates kneel or bow their heads. The sponsors each place a hand upon the shoulder of their candidate.

One of the catechists says

Let the candidate(s) for Baptism now receive the Lord's Prayer from the Church.

Celebrant

As our Savior Christ	As our Savior Christ
has taught us	has taught us,
we are bold to say,	we now pray,

People and Celebrant

Our Father, who art in heaven,   Our Father in heaven,
  hallowed be thy Name,   hallowed be your Name,
  thy kingdom come,   your kingdom come,
  thy will be done,   your will be done
    on earth as it is in heaven.   on earth as in heaven.
Give us this day our daily bread.   Give us today our daily brea
And forgive us our trespasses,   Forgive us our sins
  as we forgive those   as we forgive those
    who trespass against us.   who sin against us.
And lead us not into temptation,   Save us from the time of tri
  but deliver us from evil.   and deliver us from evil.
For thine is the kingdom,   For the kingdom, the power
  and the power, and the glory,   and the glory are yours,
  for ever and ever. Amen.   now and for ever. Amen.

The Celebrant concludes (dismissal of the candidates is optional)

(Candidate(s) go in peace.) May the Lord remain with you always. Amen.

Candidates and sponsors are dismissed, or return to their places in the congregation.

A Vigil on the Eve of Baptism

When it is desired to celebrate a vigil on the eve of the Bishops Visitation or other occasion in preparation for the administration of baptism at a principal Sunday morning service, the following order may be used.

The Vigil begins with the Service of Light, Prayer Book page 109, and continues, after the Phos hilaron, with the Salutation and Collect. Three or more of the appointed Lessons are read before the Gospel, each followed by a period of silence and a Psalm, Canticle, or hymn.

If the Vigil takes place on the eve of Pentecost, All Saints' Day or the Sunday following, or the Feast of the Baptism of our Lord, the Proper Collect, Psalms, and Lessons appointed for those vigils are used. On other occasions any appropriate Collect may be selected, and the Readings chosen from among the following:

The Story of the Flood
Genesis (7:1-5,11-18); 8:6-18; 9:8-13

Psalm 25:3-9, *or* Psalm 46

The Story of the Covenant
Exodus 19:1-9a,16-20a; 20:18-20

Canticle 2 or 13

Salvation Offered Freely to All
Isaiah 55:1-11

Canticle 9

A New Heart and a New Spirit
Ezekiel 36:24-28

Psalm 42

The Valley of Dry Bones
Ezekiel 37:1-14

Psalm 30 *or* Psalm 143

Baptized into his Death
Romans 6:3-5

or **We are Children of God**
Romans 8:14-17

or **Now is the Day of Salvation**
2 Corinthians 5:17-20

The Baptism of Jesus
Mark 1:1-6

or **You Must be Born Again**
John 3:1-6

or **The Resurrection and the Great Commission**
Matthew 28:1-10,16-20

After the Gospel (and homily) the candidates and their sponsors are called forward. The candidates kneel or bow their heads. The Sponsors each place a hand upon the shoulder of their candidate. The Celebrant then lays a hand on the head of each candidate in silence.

The Celebrant then says one of the following forms of prayer, after which a hymn may be sung. The service then concludes with a blessing or dismissal, or both.

Form 1

Holy Trinity, one God, be present at the font *tomorrow* for the sake of *these* your *servants*. Amen.

At the invocation of your great Name, let the life-giving Spirit sanctify the waters. *Amen.*

There let the old Adam be buried, and the new be raised up. *Amen.*

There let the power of evil be broken, and the power of the Spirit be revealed. *Amen.*

Strip from *these* your *servants* the soiled and tattered garb of sin, and clothe *them* with the shining robe of immortality. *Amen.*

Help *them* to know that all who are baptized into Christ have put on Christ. *Amen.*

Let *them* and all who, at the font, renounce Satan and every evil power, receive strength to overcome temptation. *Amen.*

Whoever there confesses you as Lord, acknowledge, O Lord, in your kingdom. *Amen.*

Lead them with joy from the font to the altar, and prepare for them a place at your heavenly banquet. *Amen.*

Banish from them the fear of death, and give them a sure faith in your promises. *Amen.*

Teach them to deny themselves for the sake of your Gospel, that they may never lose you, their everlasting treasure. *Amen.*

Let every one who is dedicated to you through the ministry of your holy Church be bound to you for ever, and everlastingly rewarded. *Amen.*

Grant this in your mercy, O God, for you are the ruler over all, and you live and are blessed for evermore. *Amen.*

Form 2

Lord Jesus Christ, you desire that everyone who follows you shall be born again by water and the Spirit:

Remember your *servants* [N.N.] who tomorrow are to be baptized in your Name.

By *their names* Lord:

Grant that you will know *them*, and call *them* to a life of service. *Amen.*

Grant that *they* may become the *persons* you created *them* to be. *Amen.*

Grant that *they* may be written for ever in your Book of Life. *Amen.*

Through the water of *their* baptism, Lord:

Grant that *they* may be united with you in your death. *Amen.*

Grant that *they* may receive forgiveness for all *their* sins. *Amen.*

Grant that *they* may have power to endure, and strength to have victory in the battle of life. *Amen.*

As *members* of your Church, Lord:

Grant that *they* may rise to a new life in the fellowship of those who love you. *Amen.*

Grant that *they* may suffer when another suffers, and when another rejoices, rejoice. *Amen.*

Grant that *they* may be your faithful *soldiers* and *servants* until *their* life's end. *Amen.*

Through the abiding presence of your Spirit, Lord:

Grant that *they* may lead the rest of *their lives* according to this beginning. *Amen.*

Grant that when *they pass* through the dark waters of death, you will be with *them. Amen.*

Grant that *they* may inherit the kingdom of glory prepared for *them* from the foundation of the world. *Amen.*

To you, Lord Christ, with the Father and the Holy Spirit, be honor and glory in the Church, now and for ever. *Amen.*

Concerning Reaffirmation of Baptismal Vows

This series of rites and stages of preparation employs a process similar to that of the catechumenate to prepare mature baptized persons to reaffirm their baptismal covenant and receive the laying on of hands by the bishop. It is also appropriate for already confirmed persons who wish to enter a time of disciplined renewal of the baptismal covenant and for those who have transferred into a new congregation. This process may also be used for returning persons who have been separated from the church due to notorious sins. Care, however, should be taken in distinguishing such "penitents" from the other persons in this process, in the preservation of confidentiality, and the penitent's own participation in the process conducted with pastoral sensitivity.

It is important to note, however, that this is not the catechumenate, which is appropriate only for the unbaptized. In some congregations, it may be desirable, due to limited resources, for catechumens and the previously baptized to attend meetings together during each stage. Care should be taken, however, to underscore the full and complete Christian membership of the baptized. For this reason, the rites of the catechumenate are not appropriate for them. During meetings, prayers offered for the baptized should acknowledge their baptism. Good examples of such prayers are found in the weekday collects for the Great Fifty Days of Easter in *Lesser Feasts and Fasts*. When they join the catechumens in their meetings, the baptized may appropriately be considered as assisting the catechists.

There are three stages of preparation and formation, each concluding with a rite as a transition. (The first rite, however, is used only for those baptized members who are returning to the church from a period of inactivity and for those coming from other traditions.) A final period after the third rite leads to the Reaffirmation of the Baptismal Covenant at the Easter Vigil and the presentation of the candidate to the bishop for Confirmation, Reception, or Commitment to Christian Service during the Great Fifty Days of Easter. Throughout, the candidate is valued by the community as a living example of our common need to reexamine and reaffirm our baptismal covenant, and as a model of conversion.

Lastly, the rites attempt to make full use of the existing symbolic language of the liturgy, through the use of actions and physical symbols as well as words.

Stage One. A period of inquiry designed for story sharing and to give persons enough information about Christian faith and practice and the life of the local community so they may determine if they wish to enter a disciplined period of mature formation in the story of God's saving deeds, prayer, worship, and service. At the conclusion of this period, one or more sponsors are chosen from the local congregation.

[
RITE ONE   Page 139
Welcoming Returning Members and Members Baptized in other Traditions
]

Stage Two. This is a longer period during which those being formed, along with sponsors, catechists, and other members of the community engage in deeper exploration of faith and ministry.

This formation period is based on a pattern of experience followed by reflection. The baptized persons explore the meanings of baptism and the baptismal covenant, while discerning the type of service to which God calls them in the context of the local community. The sponsors and catechists in turn train and support them in that service and help them to reflect theologically on their experience of ministry through the study of Scripture, in prayer, and in worship. Substantial periods of time are spent doing ministry and reflecting on it with catechists and sponsors.

Baptized candidates take part in the Eucharist, including the reception of Holy Communion, unless prevented by penitential discipline.

This rite is used for baptized persons who are returning to active church life after having lived apart from the Church. It is also appropriate for persons coming into this Church from another tradition.

Active baptized members of this Church simply enter the second stage without any rite although prayer may be offered in the context of this rite for "other members of this Church who are preparing to reaffirm their baptismal covenant."

RITE TWO   Page 141
Enrollment for Lenten Preparation

Stage Three. This is a stage of immediate preparation for Reaffirmation of the Baptismal Covenant at the Easter Vigil. The candidates focus on the Lenten disciplines and their role in ministry to others. In their group meetings, candidates for reaffirmation share their ongoing experience of conversion—especially with those catechumens who are preparing for baptism—and explore more deeply the life of prayer and ministry.

RITE THREE   Page 144
Maundy Thursday Rite of Preparation for the Paschal Holy Days

The baptized reaffirm their baptismal covenant at the Easter Vigil. It is appropriate for them to join those baptized at the same Vigil in the post-baptismal catechesis during the Great Fifty Days of Easter. If the Bishop was not present at the Vigil, the baptized are presented to the Bishop for the laying on of hands, preferably during the Great Fifty Days as appropriate.

Preparation of Baptized Persons for Reaffirmation of the Baptismal Covenant

Welcoming Returning Members and Members Baptized in Other Traditions

This rite is used at the principal Sunday Eucharist. It is provided for baptized persons who have returned to the life of the Church after a time away and for members baptized in other traditions. Those who wish to pursue a disciplined exploration of the implications of Christian living are recognized by the community and welcomed to begin this process.

During the Prayers of the People, those about to be welcomed are prayed for by name.

After the Prayers of the People, the senior warden or other representative of the community presents the baptized to the celebrant with these or other words:

N., We present to you these persons (or N., N.,) who are baptized members of the Body of Christ and we welcome them to our community as they undertake a process of growth in the meaning of their baptism.

Celebrant	*(to each baptized person)* What do you seek?
Answer	Renewal of my life in Christ.

Celebrant	In baptism, you died with Christ Jesus to the forces of evil and rose to new life as members of his Body. Will you study the promises made at your baptism, and strive to keep them in the fellowship of this community and the rest of the Church?
Answer	I will, with God's help.

Celebrant	Will you attend the worship of God regularly with us, to hear God's word and to celebrate the mystery of Christ's dying and rising?
Answer	I will, with God's help.

Celebrant	Will you participate in a life of service to those who are poor, outcast, or powerless?
Answer	I will, with God's help.

Celebrant	Will you strive to recognize the gifts that God has given you and discern how they are to be used in the building up of God's reign of peace and justice?
Answer	I will, with God's help.

Celebrant	*(to the sponsors/companions/friends)* You have been chosen by this communityto serve as companions to these persons. Will you support them by prayer and example and help them to grow in the knowledge and love of God?
Sponsors	We will, with God's help.

Celebrant	*(to the congregation)* Will you who witness this new beginning keep (N., N.) in your prayers and help them, share with them your ministry, bear their burdens, and forgive and encourage them?
People	We will, with God's help.

Those being presented remain standing. The sponsors place a hand on their shoulders.

Celebrant   *(extending both hands toward the baptized)* Blessed are you, our God, our Maker, for you form us in your image and restore us in Jesus Christ. In baptism, N., N., were buried with Christ and rose to new life in him. Renew them in your Holy Spirit, that they may grow as members of Christ. Strengthen their union with the rest of his Body as they join us in our life of praise and service; through our Savior, Jesus Christ, who lives and reigns with you and the Holy Spirit, now and for ever.

All   Amen.

In full view of all, the baptized write their names in the church's register of baptized persons. The deacon or a sponsor calls out the names as they are written.

Celebrant   Please welcome the new members of the community.

People   We recognize you as members of the household of God. Confess the faith of Christ crucified, proclaim his resurrection, and share with us in his eternal priesthood.

The service continues with the Peace. It is appropriate for the new members to greet as many of the faithful as possible. Some may also read the lessons, present the Bread and Wine, and perform other liturgical functions for which they have been previously qualified.

Enrollment for Lenten Preparation

This rite is used at the principal service on Ash Wednesday, In it, baptized persons who have been exploring the implications of their

*baptismal covenant and are preparing to reaffirm it at the coming
Easter Vigil are recognized as examples of conversion for the
congregation in its journey towards Easter.*

*After the Blessing of the Ashes and before their imposition, the senior
warden or other representative of the congregation presents the
baptized to the celebrant with these or other words:*

> N., we present to you N., N., who have been
> growing in an understanding of their call as
> Christians among us and now desire to undertake
> a more intense preparation to renew their
> baptismal covenant this coming Easter.

Celebrant Have they studied the promises made at their
baptism and strived to keep them in fellowship
with this community and the rest of the Church?

Sponsors They have.

Celebrant Have they attended worship regularly to hear
God's word and to celebrate the mystery of
Christ's dying and rising?

Sponsors They have.

Celebrant Have they participated in a life of service to those
who are poor, outcast, or powerless?

Sponsors They have.

Celebrant Have they strived to recognize the gifts that God
has given them and to discern how they are to be
used in the building up of God's reign of peace and
justice?

Sponsors They have.

Celebrant *(to the baptized)* Will you strive to set an example for
us (and especially for those among us who are
preparing for baptism) of that turning towards
Jesus Christ which marks true conversion?

Answer We will, with God's help.

Celebrant   *(to the sponsors)* Will you accompany these
candidates in their journey to conversion and help
them to renew their commitment to Christ?

Sponsors   We will, with God's help.

*In full view of the congregation, those enrolled kneel or bow their
heads. Their sponsors stand behind them and place a hand on their
shoulders.*

Celebrant   *(extending both hands towards the candidates)* Blessed are
you, our God, our Maker, for you faithfully call us
to return to you and do not abandon us to our
own selfishness. You have given N., N., to us as
examples of our reliance on you. Renew your
Holy Spirit in them that they may lead us in our
turning back to you as they prepare to celebrate
with us Christ's passage from death to life, who
lives and reigns with you and the Holy Spirit, one
God, now and for ever.

Answer   Amen.

The candidates stand.

Celebrant   Receive ashes as a symbol of repentance and
conversion and show us by your example how to
turn to Christ.

*The Celebrant imposes ashes on the candidates using the words of
imposition on page 265 of the Book of Common Prayer.*

*The candidates join the celebrant in imposing ashes on the
congregation.*

The second Preface of Lent is used.

*During the Lenten season, those enrolled are prayed for by name at the
Prayers of the People, separately from any catechumens.*

Maundy Thursday Rite of Preparation for the Paschal Holy Days

This rite is used at the principal service on Maundy Thursday.

If there are penitents they will have taken part in the Reconciliation of a Penitent or other appropriate ministry in which they are assured of God's pardon before participating in this rite.

When this rite is used, the appropriate Gospel is John 13: 1-15. Before the foot-washing ceremony, those preparing for reaffirmation and their sponsors stand before the celebrant in full view of the congregation.

The celebrant addresses the people in the following form rather than the form on page 93 of this book.

Celebrant   *(to those preparing for reaffirmation and their sponsors)* N., N., you have been setting an example for us of that true turning to God which lies at the heart of our Christian calling. Tonight we welcome you to join us as disciples of Jesus Christ by imitating his example and dedicating ourselves to service among us in this community. Christ Jesus came among us not to be served but to serve. Tonight we wash your feet as a sign of the servanthood to which Christ has called us and we ask you in turn to join us in this symbol of our discipleship. N., N., are you prepared to join us in our life of service?

Candidates   We are prepared.

The service continues with a rite of reconciliation, beginning on page 450 of the Book of Common Prayer with the words, "Now, in the presence of Christ. . ." omitting the confession of particular sins ("Especially..."). The Celebrant lays a hand on each one while saying the first form of absolution ("Our Lord Jesus Christ, who offered. . .").*

Their feet are washed. When all are ready, the celebrant distributes basins, ewers, and towels to them, saying to each:

Celebrant   May Christ strengthen you in the service which he lays upon
you.

They in turn wash the feet of other members of the congregation.

*The service continues with the Prayers of the People and the Peace.
If a Confession of Sin is to be used in this service it takes place at the
beginning using the Penitential Order on page 319 or page 351 in the
Book of Common Prayer.*

Celebration for a Home

The celebrant, members of the household, and friends assemble in the living room of the home (in which a table has been prepared for the Holy Communion).

The Celebrant greets the people.

The service may begin with the following or some other appropriate Collect, the Celebrant first saying

	The Lord be with you.
People	And also with you.
Celebrant	Let us pray.

Almighty and everlasting God, grant to this home the grace of your presence, that you may be known to be the inhabitant of this dwelling, and the defender of this household; through Jesus Christ our Lord, who with you and the Holy Spirit lives and reigns, one God, for ever and ever. *Amen.*

One or both of the following Lessons, or other appropriate Readings, may follow

Old Testament   Genesis 18:1-8
Epistle   3 John 1-6a,11,13-15

Between the Readings, or after the Reading if only one is used, Psalm 112:1-7, or some other psalm or song, may be sung or said.

If there is to be a Communion, a passage from the Gospel is always included. The following are appropriate:

Gospel John 11:5; 12:1-3 *or* Matthew 6:25-33

A homily or brief address may follow.

When appropriate, the Celebrant then says the following invocation

Let the mighty power of the Holy God be present in this place to banish from it every unclean spirit, to cleanse it from every residue of evil, and to make it a secure habitation for *those* who *dwell* in it; in the Name of Jesus Christ our Lord. *Amen.*

If convenient, prayers for the several rooms of the house are offered at this time. The Celebrant, with members of the household (one of them carrying a lighted candle if desired), and others as convenient, move from room to room, concluding the procession in the living room. Meanwhile, those not participating in the procession remain in the living room, praying silently or singing hymns or other suitable songs.

If the procession does not take place here, the service continues with the Blessing of the Home on page 154. The prayers in the separate rooms may be used before or after the service.

The prayers in the rooms may be used in any convenient sequence.

The appointed antiphons may be read or sung by all, or by the celebrant, or by some other person.

At the Entrance

Antiphon

Behold, I stand at the door and knock, says the Lord. If you hear my voice and open the door, I will come into the house, and eat with you, and you with me.

V. The Lord shall watch over your going out and your coming in:
R. From this time forth for evermore.

Let us pray. *(Silence)*

Sovereign Lord, you are Alpha and Omega, the beginning and the end: Send your *servants* out from this place on many errands, be *their* constant companion in the way, and welcome *them* upon their return, so that coming and going *they* may be sustained by your presence, O Christ our Lord. *Amen.*

In an Oratory or Chapel, or at a Shrine

Antiphon

Let them make me a sanctuary, that I may dwell in their midst.

V. Lift up your hands in the holy place:
R. And bless the Lord.

Let us pray. *(Silence)*

Almighty God, from you comes every good prayer, and you pour out on those who desire it the spirit of grace and supplication: Deliver your *servants* when *they draw* near to you in this place from coldness of heart and wanderings of mind, that with steadfast thoughts and kindled affections *they* may worship you in spirit and in truth; through Jesus Christ our Lord. *Amen.*

In a Study or Library

Antiphon

Teach us, O Lord, where wisdom is to be found, and show us the place of understanding.

V.   Seek the Lord your God, and you will find him:
R.   Search for him with all your heart and with all your soul.

Let us pray. *(Silence)*

O God of truth, eternal ground of all that is, beyond space and time yet within them, transcending all things yet pervading them: Show yourself to us, for we go about in ignorance; reveal yourself to us, for it is you that we seek, O Triune God, Father, Son, and Holy Spirit. *Amen.*

In a Bedroom

Antiphon

Guide us waking, O Lord, and guard us sleeping, that awake we may watch with Christ, and asleep we may rest in peace.

V.   I lie down and go to sleep:
R.   I wake again, because the Lord sustains me.

Celebration for a Home   149

Let us pray. *(Silence)*

O God of life and love, the true rest of your people: Sanctify to your *servants their* hours of rest and refreshment, *their* sleeping and *their* waking; and grant that, strengthened by the indwelling of the Holy Spirit, *they* may rise to serve you all the days of *their* life; through Jesus Christ our Lord. *Amen.*

In a Child's Room

Antiphon

Jesus said, Let the children come to me, and do not hinder them; for to those like them belongs the kingdom of heaven.

V. Praise the Lord, you children of the Lord:
R. Praise the Name of the Lord.

Let us pray. *(Silence)*

Heavenly Father, your Son our Savior took young children into his arms and blessed them: Embrace the *child* whose room this is with your unfailing love, protect *him* from all danger, and bring *him* in safety to each new day, until *he greets* with joy the great day of your kingdom; through Jesus Christ our Lord. *Amen.*

In a Guest Room

Antiphon

Do not neglect to show hospitality, for thereby some have entertained angels unawares.

V. Open your homes to each other without complaining:
R. Use the gifts you have received from God for the good of others.

Let us pray. *(Silence)*

Loving God, you have taught us to welcome one another as Christ welcomed us: Bless those who from time to time share the hospitality of this home. May your fatherly care shield them, the love of your dear Son preserve them from all evil, and the guidance of your Holy Spirit keep them in the way that leads to eternal life; through Jesus Christ our Lord. *Amen.*

In a Bathroom

Antiphon

I will sprinkle you with clean water, and you will be cleansed.

V. Let us hold fast the confession of our hope without wavering:
R. Having our bodies washed with pure water.

Let us pray. *(Silence)*

O holy God, in the incarnation of your Son our Lord you made our flesh the instrument of your self-revelation: Give us a proper respect and reverence for our mortal bodies, keeping them clean and fair, whole and sound; that, glorifying you in them, we may confidently await our being clothed upon with spiritual bodies, when that which is mortal is transformed by life; through Jesus Christ our Lord. *Amen.*

In a Workroom or Workshop

Antiphon

Many there are who rely upon their hands and are skillful in their own work.

V. Prosper, O Lord, the work of our hands:
R. Prosper our handiwork.

Let us pray. *(Silence)*

O God, your blessed Son worked with his hands in the carpenter shop in Nazareth: Be present, we pray, with *those* who *work* in this place, that, laboring as *workers* together with you, *they* may share the joy of your creation; through Jesus Christ our Lord. *Amen.*

In the Kitchen

Antiphon

You shall eat in plenty and be satisfied, and praise the Name of the Lord your God, who has dealt wondrously with you.

V. The eyes of all wait upon you, O Lord:
R. And you give them their food in due season.

Let us pray. *(Silence)*

O Lord our God, you supply every need of ours according to your great riches: Bless the hands that work in this place, and give us grateful hearts for daily bread; through Jesus Christ our Lord. *Amen.*

In a Dining Room or Area

Antiphon

The living God gave you from heaven rain and fruitful seasons, satisfying your hearts with food and gladness.

V. He brings forth food from the earth,
   and wine to gladden our hearts:
R. Oil to make a cheerful countenance,
   and bread to strengthen the heart.

Let us pray. *(Silence)*

Blessed are you, O Lord, King of the universe, for you give us food and drink to sustain our lives: Make us grateful for all your mercies, and mindful of the needs of others; through Jesus Christ our Lord. *Amen.*

In a Terrace or Garden

Antiphon

As the earth puts forth its blossom, or bushes in a garden burst into flower, so shall the Lord God make righteousness and praise blossom before all the nations.

V. My boundaries enclose a pleasant land:
R. Indeed, I have a goodly heritage.

Let us pray. *(Silence)*

Jesus, our good Companion, on many occasions you withdrew with your friends for quiet and refreshment: Be present with your *servants* in this place, to which *they come* for fellowship and recreation; and make of it, we pray, a place of serenity and peace; in your Name we ask it. *Amen.*

In the Living Room or Family Room

Antiphon

Oh, how good and pleasant it is, when God's people live together in unity!

V. Above everything, love one another earnestly:
R. For love covers many sins.

Let us pray. *(Silence)*

Give your blessing, Lord, to all who share this room, that they may be knit together in fellowship here on earth, and joined with the communion of your saints in heaven; through Jesus Christ our Lord. *Amen.*

In those rooms and other places for which no provision has been made in this service, any suitable antiphon, versicle, and prayer may be used.

The Blessing of the Home

When the procession has returned to the living room, or immediately after the homily (and invocation), the Celebrant completes the blessing of the home as follows:

Antiphon

The effect of righteousness will be peace, and the result of righteousness tranquility and trust for ever. My people will abide in secure dwellings and in quiet resting places.

V. Unless the Lord builds the house:
R. Their labor is in vain who build it.

Let us pray. *(Silence)*

Visit, O blessed Lord, this home with the gladness of your presence. Bless *all* who *live* here with the gift of your love; and grant that *they* may manifest your love [to each other and] to all whose lives *they touch.* May *they* grow in grace and in the knowledge and love of you; guide, comfort, and strengthen *them*; and preserve *them* in peace, O Jesus Christ, now and for ever. *Amen.*

The Celebrant then says to the people

The peace of the Lord be always with you.
And also with you.

The People greet one another in the name of the Lord.

If there is not to be a Communion, the service concludes with the Lord's Prayer and a blessing.

If there is to be a Communion, the Liturgy continues with the Offertory.

Members of the household present the offerings of bread and wine.

The Celebrant continues with one of the authorized Eucharistic Prayers, or with one of the Forms of the Great Thanksgiving from An Order for Celebrating the Holy Eucharist.

If the Great Thanksgiving provides for a Proper Preface, the following may be used

Through Jesus Christ our Lord, who grew to perfect manhood in his parents' home at Nazareth, and in the home of friends in Bethany revealed himself as Life and Resurrection.

In place of the usual postcommunion prayer, the following may be used

How wonderful you are, O gracious God, in all your dealings with your people! We praise you now, and give you thanks, because in the blessed Sacrament of the Body and Blood of our Savior Jesus Christ you have visited this house and hallowed it by your presence. Stay among us, we pray, to bind us together in your love and peace. May we serve you, and others in your name; through Jesus Christ our Lord. *Amen.*

The service may conclude with a dismissal.

If there has not been a Communion as part of the service, it is desirable that there be a celebration of the Holy Eucharist in the home at the earliest convenient time.

Blessing of a Pregnant Woman

The following may be used either privately or at a public service.

O Lord and giver of life, receive our prayer for N. and for the child she has conceived, that they may happily come to the time of birth, and serving you in all things may rejoice in your loving providence. We ask this through our Lord Jesus Christ, who lives and reigns with you and the Holy Spirit, one God, now and for ever. *Amen.*

When appropriate, any or all of the following may be added:

Blessed are you, Lord God. You have blessed the union of N. and N. *Amen.*

Blessed are you, Lord God. May your blessing be upon N. and the child she carries. *Amen.*

Blessed are you, Lord God. May this time of pregnancy be for N. and N. months of drawing nearer to you and to one another. *Amen.*

Blessed are you, Lord God. May N. and N.'s experience of birth be full of awe and wonder and the joy of sharing in your creation. *Amen.*

Blessed are you, Lord God. Let the fullness of your blessing be upon those whom we bless in your Name: Father, Son, and Holy Spirit. *Amen.*

The anticipation of birth is an appropriate time for the Minister of the Congregation to discuss with expectant parents the meaning of Baptism.

The Preparation of Parents and Godparents for the Baptism of Infants and Young Children

Concerning the Service

This process is designed to deepen the Christian formation of those who will present infants and young children for baptism. Its division into stages—each concluding with a rite—parallels the form of the catechumenate. It is essential, however, that these persons be distinguished from the catechumens except when they may be themselves preparing for baptism, and therefore catechumens.

Stage One. This stage begins as soon as the parents discover the pregnancy. In consultation with the pastor, they choose godparents. The godparents must be baptized persons and at least one a member of the local community. A schedule of meetings throughout the pregnancy is planned. This is a brief stage, leading shortly to the first rite.

RITE ONE
The Blessing of Parents at the Beginning of the Pregnancy

This rite "The Blessing of a Pregnant Woman," appears on page 157. In order to more strongly indicate the role of the father, the following changes should be made, in addition to changing the title. (If the father is not present or not involved, the rite follows the form for a woman, omitting the father's name in the prayers.)

In the opening prayer, the father's name as well as the mother's is used, and "they" replaces "she."

After the fourth petition is added:

Blessed are you, our God. May N. and N., along with their child's godparents, N. and N. (and N. and N., their other children), find their faith deepened and their ministry strengthened as they prepare for this child's birth and baptism. *Amen.*

This rite takes place at the Sunday Eucharist after the Prayers of the People. It is followed by the Peace.

Stage Two. This period consists of the remainder of the pregnancy and the time of birth. During this stage, the parents, their other children, and the godparents meet regularly with one or more catechists to deepen their formation in salvation history, prayer, worship, and social ministry. Its educational pattern is one of experience followed by reflection. In their daily lives, participants find ample resources for reflection upon the ways in which their own baptismal covenant is being lived within their vocation of marriage, family and child-bearing. They also explore prayer and worship in the home as an extension of the liturgy of the Church and in the context of the Church Year, and they grow in an understanding of the household as a domestic manifestation of the People of God whose life together is part of the history of salvation.

If a parent is a catechumen, this process takes place within the catechumenate. A baptized spouse may serve to sponsor the catechumen.

RITE TWO
Thanksgiving for the Birth or Adoption of a Child

This rite is found in the Book of Common Prayer (pages 439-445). Of the final prayers, the prayer "For a child not yet baptized" (page 444) is appropriate. The celebrant signs the infant with the cross and announces the date of the baptism. Henceforth the child is prayed for by name at the Prayers of the People, until the baptismal day.

Stage Three. In this period of preparation for baptism, the parents and godparents continue to meet with the catechist(s). Couples or individuals who have raised children in the Church may be helpful as resources or catechists, as may be others who have completed this process previously. The experience of parenthood furnishes new challenges to faith and ministry upon which reflection will be fruitful. The process of family life, sharing in the congregation's life of worship, and ministry to others will find new shape with the advent of the new child.

This is also a time to explore more fully the responsibilities that the parents and godparents will accept at the baptism. They explore topics such as: the best way to interpret the meaning of the Eucharist to a child partaking of it in his or her growing years; how to model ministry and prayer for the growing child; and ways of introducing the child to the story of salvation. The role of the godparents is also more fully developed.

[
RITE THREE   Book of Common Prayer, Page 299
Holy Baptism
]

In accordance with the Book of Common Prayer, this will take place on a major baptismal day at a principal service of worship. The infant will be signed (with chrism, if desired) and may receive Holy Communion (in the form of a few drops of wine if the child is not yet weaned).

After this, the parents, godparents and congregation have the responsibility of carrying out the child's formation in salvation history, prayer, worship, and social ministry. Childhood and adolescence will be a time of formation and exploration of the mysteries of the faith, moving towards the goal of reaffirmation of the baptismal covenant at a mature age.

Those who lead this preparation process should include laity and clergy. Deacons have a special role as leaders of servant ministry, as do those who have reared children in the Church, even if they seem to have had little success. Whenever possible, the bishop should preside over the rites and take part in the teaching. The bishop will also preside at the baptism whenever possible.

Adaptation for Special Circumstances

Deferred Baptism

In the case of young children, the parents may, in consultation with the pastor of the congregation, determine to defer baptism until the child is old enough to go through the catechumenate. In such case, parents go through the same process during the pregnancy and birth, but the stages conclude not with baptism but with the admission of the child to the catechumenate (page 117). The parents and godparents should receive ongoing support in the formation of the child.

Other Adaptations

When parents present a child for baptism without having gone through this process beginning at pregnancy, the first and second stages above are combined. The first rite is dropped and the second rite is the enrollment of the child as a candidate for baptism (adapted to circumstances). After a final period of preparation (perhaps along with adult candidates), the child is baptized.

It is important to acknowledge that, if a difficulty arises during the course of the pregnancy, the godparents and catechists are the primary ministers to the parents. If the pregnancy is terminated by miscarriage, or if the baby is stillborn, these persons continue to support and assist the parents in dealing with such an event.

It should be noted that a baby with congenital deficiencies (including mental or learning disabilities) should be baptized. In cases where it seems necessary to perform an emergency baptism, the sponsoring group supports the parents. If the infant survives, the formative period may continue and the formal celebration of the baptism takes place on a major baptismal day.

Anniversary of a Marriage

This form is intended for use in the context of a celebration of the Holy Eucharist. When the form is used at a principal service on a Sunday or Major Holy Day, the Proper of the Day is used. When it is used at other times, the Psalm and Lessons are selected from those recommended for use at the Celebration and Blessing of a Marriage, and one of the following Collects is used for the Collect of the Day.

O gracious and everliving God, look mercifully on N. and N., who come to renew the promises they have made to each other. Grant them your blessing, and assist them with your grace, that with true fidelity and steadfast love they may honor and keep their promises and vows; through Jesus Christ our Savior, who lives and reigns with you, in the unity of the Holy Spirit, one God, for ever and ever. *Amen.*

or this

O God, you have so consecrated the covenant of marriage that in it is represented the spiritual unity between Christ and his Church: Send your blessing upon N. and N., who come to renew their promises to each other, and grant them your grace, that they may so love, honor, and cherish each other in faithfulness and patience, in wisdom and true godliness, that their lives together may be a witness to your love and forgiveness, and that their home may be a haven of blessing and peace; through Jesus Christ our Lord, who lives and reigns with you and the Holy Spirit, one God, now and for ever. *Amen.*

or this

Grant, O God, in your compassion, that N. and N., having taken each other in marriage, and affirming again the covenant which they have made, may grow in forgiveness, loyalty, and love; and come at last to the eternal joys which you have promised through Jesus Christ our Lord; who lives and reigns with you, in the unity of the Holy Spirit, one God, for ever and ever. *Amen.*

Immediately after the Sermon (and the Creed if appointed), the Husband and Wife present themselves before the celebrant, who stands facing the people.

All stand, and the Celebrant addresses the congregation with these or similar words

Friends in Christ, we are gathered together with N. and N., who have come today to give thanks to God for his blessing upon their marriage, and to reaffirm their marriage covenant.

The Celebrant then asks the man

N., do you here, in the presence of God and of this congregation, renew the promises you made when you bound yourself to N. in holy matrimony?

The Man answers

I do.

The Celebrant then asks the woman

N., do you here, in the presence of God and of this congregation, renew the promises you made when you bound yourself to N. in holy matrimony?

The Woman answers

I do.

The Husband and Wife, kneeling or standing, say together

We thank you, most gracious God, for consecrating our marriage in Christ's Name and presence. Lead us further in companionship with each other and with you. Give us grace to live together in love and fidelity, with care for one another. Strengthen us all our days, and bring us to that holy table where, with those we love, we will feast for ever in our heavenly home; through Jesus Christ our Lord. *Amen.*

The Celebrant then blesses them, saying

May God the Father, who at creation ordained that man and woman become one flesh, keep you one. *Amen.*

May God the Son, who adorned this manner of life by his first miracle, at the wedding in Cana of Galilee, be present with you always. *Amen.*

May God the Holy Spirit, who has given you the will to persevere in your love and in your covenant with each other, strengthen your bond. *Amen.*

And may God the Holy Trinity, the source of all unity, bless you this day and for ever. *Amen.*

The service continues with the Peace, or, at a principal service, with the Prayers of the People.

The husband and wife may present the bread and wine at the Offertory.

If there is not to be a Communion, the service concludes with the Lord's Prayer and the Peace.

When this form is used as an act of reconciliation, the celebrant may adapt it in consultation with the parties.

A Public Service of Healing

The service begins as appointed for a celebration of the Holy Eucharist, or with the Penitential Order, or with the following greeting

Celebrant	Grace and peace be with you, from God our Father and the Lord Jesus Christ.
People	And also with you.
Celebrant	Let us pray.

The Celebrant says this or some other appropriate Collect

O God of peace, you have taught us that in returning and rest we shall be saved, in quietness and confidence shall be our strength: By the might of your Spirit lift us, we pray, to your presence, where we may be still and know that you are God; through Jesus Christ our Lord, who with you and the Holy Spirit lives and reigns, one God, for ever and ever. *Amen.*

One or two Lessons are read before the Gospel.

Between the Lessons, and before the Gospel, a Psalm, hymn, or anthem may be sung or said.

If the Proper of the Day is not used, the Lessons, Psalm, and Gospel are selected from the Table on page 171-173.

A sermon or meditation, or a period of silence, or both, may follow the Gospel.

The service continues with the Creed, or with the Prayers of the People.

For the Prayers of the People a Litany of Healing, as follows, may be used.

Litany of Healing

The Celebrant introduces the Litany with this bidding

Let us name before God those for whom we offer our prayers.

The People audibly name those for whom they are interceding.

A Person appointed then leads the Litany

God the Father, your will for all people is health and salvation;
We praise you and thank you, O Lord.

God the Son, you came that we might have life, and might have it more abundantly;
We praise you and thank you, O Lord.

God the Holy Spirit, you make our bodies the temple of your presence;
We praise you and thank you, O Lord.

Holy Trinity, one God, in you we live and move and have our being;
We praise you and thank you, O Lord.

Lord, grant your healing grace to all who are sick, injured, or disabled, that they may be made whole;
Hear us, O Lord of life.

Grant to all who seek your guidance, and to all who are lonely, anxious, or despondent, a knowledge of your will and an awareness of your presence;
Hear us, O Lord of life.

Mend broken relationships, and restore those in emotional distress to soundness of mind and serenity of spirit;
Hear us, O Lord of life.

Bless physicians, nurses, and all others who minister to the suffering, granting them wisdom and skill, sympathy and patience;
Hear us, O Lord of life.

Grant to the dying peace and a holy death, and uphold by the grace and consolation of your Holy Spirit those who are bereaved;
Hear us, O Lord of life.

Restore to wholeness whatever is broken by human sin, in our lives, in our nation, and in the world;
Hear us, O Lord of life.

You are the Lord who does wonders:
You have declared your power among the peoples.

With you, O Lord, is the well of life:
And in your light we see light.

Hear us, O Lord of life:
Heal us, and make us whole.

Let us pray.

A period of silence follows.

*The Celebrant concludes the Prayers with one of the following or some
other suitable Collect:*

Almighty God, giver of life and health: Send your blessing
on all who are sick, and upon those who minister to them,
that all weakness may be vanquished by the triumph of the
risen Christ; who lives and reigns for ever and ever. *Amen.*

or this

Heavenly Father, you have promised to hear what we ask in
the Name of your Son: Accept and fulfill our petitions, we
pray, not as we ask in our ignorance, nor as we deserve in
our sinfulness, but as you know and love us in your Son
Jesus Christ our Lord. *Amen.*

or this

O Lord our God, accept the fervent prayers of your people;
in the multitude of your mercies look with compassion upon
us and all who turn to you for help; for you are gracious, O
lover of souls, and to you we give glory, Father, Son, and
Holy Spirit, now and for ever. *Amen.*

*A Confession of Sin follows, if it has not been said at the beginning of
the service.*

*The Celebrant now invites those who wish to receive the laying on of
hands (and anointing) to come forward.*

*If oil for the anointing of the sick is to be blessed, the form on page 455
of the Prayer Book is used.*

The following anthem is sung or said

Savior of the world, by your cross and precious blood you
have redeemed us;
Save us, and help us, we humbly beseech you, O Lord.

The Celebrant says the following blessing over those who have come forward

The Almighty Lord, who is a strong tower to all who put their trust in him, to whom all things in heaven, on earth, and under the earth bow and obey: Be now and evermore your defense, and make you know and feel that the only Name under heaven given for health and salvation is the Name of our Lord Jesus Christ. *Amen.*

The Celebrant then lays hands on each person (and, having dipped a thumb in the oil of the sick, makes the sign of the cross on their foreheads), and says one of the following:

N., I lay my hands upon you [and anoint you with oil] in the Name of the Father, and of the Son, and of the Holy Spirit, beseeching our Lord Jesus Christ to sustain you with his presence, to drive away all sickness of body and spirit, and to give you that victory of life and peace which will enable you to serve him both now and evermore. *Amen.*

or this

N., I lay my hands upon you [and anoint you with oil] in the Name of our Lord and Savior Jesus Christ, beseeching him to uphold you and fill you with his grace, that you may know the healing power of his love. *Amen.*

or this

[N.,] I lay my hands upon you [and anoint you with oil] in the Name of the Father, and of the Son, and of the Holy Spirit. *Amen.*

or prayer may be offered for each person individually according to that person's need, with laying on of hands (and anointing).

Lay persons with a gift of healing may join the celebrant in the laying on of hands.

The service continues with the exchange of the Peace.

If there is not to be a Communion, the service concludes with the Lord's Prayer and the prayer and blessing given below.

If the Eucharist is to be celebrated, the Liturgy continues with the Offertory.

In place of the usual postcommunion prayer (or, if there has not been a Communion, after the Lord's Prayer), the following prayer is said

Almighty and eternal God, so draw our hearts to you, so guide our minds, so fill our imaginations, so control our wills, that we may be wholly yours, utterly dedicated to you; and then use us, we pray, as you will, and always to your glory and the welfare of your people; through our Lord and Savior Jesus Christ. *Amen.*

The Celebrant pronounces this blessing

May God the Father bless you, God the Son heal you, God the Holy Spirit give you strength. May God the holy and undivided Trinity guard your body, save your soul, and bring you safely to his heavenly country; where he lives and reigns for ever and ever. *Amen.*

A Deacon, or the Celebrant, dismisses the people.

A Table of Suggested Lessons and Psalms

Old Testament

Exodus 16:13-15 (Manna in the wilderness)
1 Kings 17:17-24 (Elijah restores the widow's son to life)
2 Kings 5:9-14 (Healing of Naaman)
2 Kings 20:1-5 (I have heard your prayer . . . I will heal you)
Isaiah 11:1-3a (The gifts of the Spirit)

Isaiah 42:1-7 (The suffering servant)
Isaiah 53:3-5 (With his stripes are we healed)
Isaiah 61:1-3 (Good tidings to the afflicted)

Psalms

Psalm 13 (My heart is joyful because of your saving help)
Psalm 20:1-6 (May the Lord answer you in the day of trouble)
Psalm 23 (You have anointed my head with oil)
Psalm 27 *or* 27:1-7,9,18 (The Lord is the strength of my life)
Psalm 91 (He will give his angels charge over you)
Psalm 103 (He forgives all your sins)
Psalm 121 (My help comes from the Lord)
Psalm 130 (My soul waits for the Lord)
Psalm 139:1-17 (Where can I go from your Spirit?)
Psalm 145:14-22 (The eyes of all wait on you, O Lord)
Psalm 146 (Happy are they who have the God of Jacob for their help)

New Testament

Acts 3:1-10 (Peter and John heal the lame man)
Acts 5:12-16 (Healings in Jerusalem; Peter's shadow)
Acts 10:36-43 (Apostolic preaching: He went about . . . healing)
Acts 16:16-18 (The slave girl with the spirit of divination)
Romans 8:18-23 (We await the redemption of our bodies)
Romans 8:31-39 (Nothing can separate us from the love of God)
2 Corinthians 1:3-5 (God comforts us in affliction)
Colossians 1:11-20 (May you be strengthened with all power)
Hebrews 12:1-2 (Looking to Jesus, the perfecter of our faith)
James 5:(13)14-16 (Is any among you sick?)
1 John 5:13-15 (That you may know that you have eternal life)

The Gospel

Matthew 9:2-8 (Your sins are forgiven)
Matthew 26:26-30,36-39 (The Last Supper: Not as I will)
Mark 1:21-28 (Jesus heals the man with the unclean spirit)
Mark 1:29-34a (Jesus heals Peter's mother-in-law and others)
Mark 5:1-20 (Healing of Gerasene demoniac)
Mark 5:22-24 (Healing of Jairus' daughter)

Mark 6:7,12-13 (They anointed with oil many that were sick)
Luke 17:11-19 (Your faith has made you well)
John 5:1b-9 (Do you want to be healed?)
John 6:47-51 (I am the bread of life)
John 9:1-11 (Healing of the man born blind)

Concerning Exorcism

The practice of expelling evil spirits by means of prayer and set formulas derives its authority from the Lord himself who identified these acts as signs of his messiahship. Very early in the life of the Church the development and exercise of such rites were reserved to the bishop, at whose discretion they might be delegated to selected presbyters and others deemed competent.

In accordance with this established tradition, those who find themselves in need of such a ministry should make the fact known to the bishop, through their parish priest, in order that the bishop may determine whether exorcism is needed, who is to perform the rite, and what prayers or other formularies are to be used.

Burial of One Who Does Not Profess the Christian Faith

This anthem; and any of the following Psalms, Lessons, and Prayers; and the form of Committal given below may be used with the Order for Burial on page 506 of the Prayer Book.

Opening Anthem

The steadfast love of the Lord never ceases,
his mercies never come to an end;
they are new every morning;
great is his faithfulness.
The Lord will not cast off for ever.
Though he cause grief, he will have compassion
according to the abundance of his steadfast love;
The Lord does not willingly afflict or grieve his children.

Lessons and Psalms

Ecclesiastes 3:1-11 (For everything there is a season)
Ecclesiastes 12:1-7 (Remember your Creator in the days of your youth)
Psalm 23 (The Lord is my shepherd)
Psalm 90 (Lord, you have been our refuge)
Psalm 121 (I lift up my eyes to the hills)
Psalm 130 (Out of the depths have I called to you, O Lord)
Romans 8:35-39 (Who shall separate us from the love of Christ?)
John 10:11-16 (I am the good shepherd)

Prayers

For the Deceased

Almighty God, we entrust all who are dear to us to your
never-failing care and love, for this life and the life to come,
knowing that you are doing for them better things than we
can desire or pray for; through Jesus Christ our Lord. *Amen.*

Into your hands, O God, we commend our *brother, N.,* as
into the hands of a faithful Creator and most loving Savior.
In your infinite goodness, wisdom, and power, work in *him*
the merciful purpose of your perfect will, through Jesus
Christ our Lord. *Amen.*

For those who mourn

O God of grace and glory, we remember before you this day
our brother (sister), *N.* We thank you for giving *him* to us,
his family and friends, to know and to love as a companion
on our earthly pilgrimage. In your boundless compassion,
console us who mourn. Give us quiet confidence that we
may continue our course in faith; through Jesus Christ our
Lord. *Amen.*

O merciful Father, you have taught us in your holy Word
that you do not willingly afflict or grieve your children:
Look with pity upon the sorrows of your servants for whom
our prayers are offered. Remember them, O Lord, in mercy,
nourish their souls with patience, comfort them with a sense
of your goodness, lift up your countenance upon them, and
give them peace; through Jesus Christ our Lord. *Amen.*

Almighty God, Father of mercies and giver of comfort: Deal graciously, we pray, with all who mourn; that, casting all their care on you, they may know the consolation of your love; through Jesus Christ our Lord. *Amen.*

Most merciful God, whose wisdom is beyond our understanding, deal graciously with *N.N.* in *their* grief. Surround *them* with your love, that *they* may not be overwhelmed by *their* loss, but have confidence in your goodness, and strength to meet the days to come; through Jesus Christ our Lord. *Amen.*

For the Christian community

Most loving Father, whose will it is for us to give thanks for all things, to fear nothing but the loss of you, and to cast all our care on you who care for us: Preserve us from faithless fears and worldly anxieties, that no clouds of this mortal life may hide from us the light of that love which is immortal, and which you have manifested to us in your Son Jesus Christ our Lord. *Amen.*

Almighty God, give us grace to cast away the works of darkness, and put on the armor of light, now in the time of this mortal life in which your Son Jesus Christ came to visit us in great humility; that in the last day, when he shall come again in his glorious majesty to judge both the living and the dead, we may rise to the life immortal; through him who lives and reigns for ever and ever. *Amen.*

The Committal

Holy God, Holy and Mighty, Holy Immortal One, have mercy upon us.

You only are immortal, the creator and maker of mankind; and we are mortal, formed of the earth, and to earth shall we return. For so did you ordain when you created me, saying, "You are dust, and to dust you shall return." All of us go down to the dust; yet even at the grave we make our song: Alleluia, alleluia, alleluia.

Holy God, Holy and Mighty, Holy Immortal One, have mercy upon us.

Commissioning for
Lay Ministries in the Church

*The Ministers of the Church are lay persons, bishops, priests, and
deacons. Lay persons are commissioned for their ministry by the
Sacrament of Holy Baptism, and no form of commissioning for special
functions is necessary. The form which follows is intended for use when
a public recognition of a special function is desired. It may be adapted
for the admission of persons to ministries not provided for in the text.*

This form may be used following the homily (and Creed) at the Eucharist, or at the time of the hymn or anthem following the Collects in Morning or Evening Prayer, or separately.

After the Examination, each group of candidates is presented separately by an appointed sponsor.

Symbols appropriate to the ministry may be given to the candidates as they are commissioned.

When the number of candidates for any office is large, it is sufficient to say the sentence of commissioning once over the entire group, but it is desirable that each person be greeted individually (and be given an appropriate symbol).

The Examination

The congregation being seated, the celebrant stands in full view of the people. The sponsors and candidates stand facing the celebrant.

The Celebrant says these or similar words

Brothers and Sisters in Christ Jesus, we are all baptized by the one Spirit into one Body, and given gifts for a variety of ministries for the common good. Our purpose is to commission *these persons* in the Name of God and of this congregation to a special ministry to which *they are* called.

The Celebrant asks the sponsor or sponsors

Are these persons you are to present prepared by a commitment to Christ as Lord, by regular attendance at worship, and by the knowledge of *their* duties, to exercise *their* ministry to the honor of God, and the well-being of his Church?

Sponsor I believe *they are.*

The Celebrant then says these or similar words

You have been called to a ministry in this congregation. Will you, as long as you are engaged in this work, perform it with diligence?

Candidate I will.

Celebrant Will you faithfully and reverently execute the duties of your ministry to the honor of God, and the benefit of the members of this congregation?

Candidate I will.

When used as a separate service, a Scripture reading from the list on page 195 (and a homily) follows here.

The Commissioning

One or more of the following forms is used as appropriate.

The appointed antiphons may be read or sung by all, or by the celebrant, or by some other person.

1. Wardens and Members of the Vestry

Sponsor I present to you *these persons* to be admitted to the ministry of Warden (Member of the Vestry) in this congregation.

Antiphon

The Lord gives wisdom; from his mouth come knowledge and understanding; he stores up sound wisdom for the upright; he is a shield to those who walk in integrity.

V.   I am your servant; grant me understanding:
R.   That I may know your decrees.

Let us pray.   *(Silence)*

O Eternal God, the foundation of all wisdom and the source of all courage: Enlighten with your grace the Wardens and Vestry of this congregation, and so rule their minds, and guide their counsels, that in all things they may seek your glory and promote the mission of your Church; through Jesus Christ our Lord. *Amen.*

In the Name of God and of this congregation. I commission you [N.] as Warden (Member of the Vestry) in this *Parish* [and give you this _____ as a token of your ministry].

2. Deputies to the General Convention or Delegates to Diocesan Convention

Sponsor I present to you *these persons*, duly elected by the people and clergy of this diocese as *Deputies* to the General Convention, to be commissioned for *their* ministry.

or the following

Sponsor	I present to you *these persons*, duly elected as *Delegates* to Diocesan Convention, to be commissioned for *their* ministry.

Antiphon

Call a solemn assembly, gather the people, assemble the elders, and sanctify the congregation.

V. Save your people, Lord, and bless your inheritance.
R. Govern and uphold them, now and always.

Let us pray. *(Silence)*

Eternal Lord God, who by the Holy Spirit presided at the council of the Apostles to guide them in all knowledge and truth: Be present with the *Deputies of this diocese soon to be assembled in General Convention.* In the passions of debate give them a quiet spirit, in the complexities of the issues give them clear minds, and in the moments of decision give them courageous hearts. Guide them in all things to seek only your glory and the good of your Church; through Jesus Christ our Lord. *Amen.*

In the Name of God and of this diocese (congregation), I commission you [N.] as *Deputies* to General Convention (*Delegates* to Diocesan Convention) [and give you this
_____ as a token of your ministry].

3. Servers at the Altar

Sponsor	I present to you *these persons* to be admitted to the ministry of Server in this congregation.

Antiphon

Do not be negligent, for the Lord has chosen you to stand in his presence, to minister to him, and to be his minister.

V.   I will go to the altar of God:
R.   To the God of my joy and gladness.

Let us pray.   *(Silence)*

O God, our gracious Father: Bless the servers of your Church that they may so serve before your earthly altar in reverence and holiness, that they may attain, with all your saints and angels, the joy of serving you and worshiping you before your Heavenly Altar; through Jesus Christ our Lord. *Amen.*

In the Name of God and of this congregation, I commission you [N.] as Server in this *Parish,* [and give you this _____ as a token of your ministry].

4. Altar Guild Members and Sacristans

Sponsor   I present to you *these persons* to be admitted to the ministry of the Altar Guild (Sacristan) in this congregation.

Antiphon

The Levites were responsible for the ark, the table, the lampstand, the altars, and the vessels of the sanctuary with which the priests minister.

V.   In the temple of the Lord all are crying, "Glory!"
R.   Holiness adorns your house, O Lord, for ever.

Let us pray. *(Silence)*

O God, you accepted the service of Levites in your temple, and your Son was pleased to accept the loving service of his friends: Bless the ministry of *these persons* and give *them* grace, that *they,* caring for the vessels and vestments of your worship and the adornment of your sanctuary, may make the place of your presence glorious; through Jesus Christ our Lord. *Amen.*

In the Name of God and of this congregation, I commission you [N.] as member of the Altar Guild (Sacristan) of this *Parish* [and give you this _____ as a token of your ministry].

5. Catechists or Teachers

Sponsor   I present to you *these persons* to be admitted to the ministry of Catechist (Teacher) in this congregation.

Antiphon

The words which I command you this day shall be upon your hearts; and you shall teach them diligently to your children, and shall talk of them when you sit in your house, and when you walk by the way, and when you lie down, and when you rise.

V.   We will recount to generations to come the praiseworthy deeds and the power of the Lord:

R.   And the wonderful works he has done.

Let us pray. *(Silence)*

God of all wisdom and knowledge, give your blessing and
guidance to all who teach in your Church, that by word and
example they may lead those whom they teach to the
knowledge and love of you; through Jesus Christ our Lord.
Amen.

In the Name of God and of this congregation, I commission
you [N.] as Catechist (Teacher) in this *Parish* [and give you
this _____ as a token of your ministry].

6. Evangelists

Sponsor   I present to you *these persons* to be admitted to
               the ministry of Evangelist in this congregation.

Antiphon

The gifts of the Lord were that some should be apostles,
some prophets, some evangelists, some pastors and teachers,
to equip the saints for the work of ministry, for building up
the body of Christ.

V.   Declare his glory among the nations
     and his wonders among the people:
R.   Tell it out among the nations: "The Lord is King!"

Let us pray.   *(Silence)*

Gracious Father, your Son before he ascended to glory
declared that your people would receive power from the
Holy Spirit to bear witness to him to the ends of the earth:
Be present with all who go forth in his Name. Let your love
shine through their witness, so that the blind may see, the
deaf hear, the lame walk, the dead be raised up, and the poor
have the good news preached to them; through Jesus Christ
our Lord. *Amen.*

In the Name of God and of this congregation, I commission
you [N.,] as Evangelist in this *Parish* [and give you this
_____ as a token of your ministry].

7. Singers

Sponsor   I present to you *these persons* to be admitted to the
              ministry of Singer (Cantor) (Chorister) in this
              congregation.

Antiphon

Sing to the Lord and bless his Name; proclaim the good
news of his salvation from day to day.

V.   Come let us sing to the Lord:
R.   Let us shout for joy to the Rock of our salvation.

Let us pray.   *(Silence)*

O God, who inspired David the King both to write songs
and to appoint singers for your worship: Give grace to the
singers in your Church, that with psalms, and hymns, and
spiritual songs, they may sing and make music to the glory
of your Name; through Jesus Christ our Lord. *Amen.*

In the Name of God and of this congregation, I commission
you [N.] as a *Singer* in this *Parish* [and give this _____
as a token of your ministry].

8. Directors of Music, Organists, and other Musicians

Sponsor   I present to you *this person* to be admitted to the ministry of *Organist and Choirmaster* in this congregation.

Antiphon

David commanded the chief of the Levites to appoint musicians who should play loudly on musical instruments, on harps and lyres and cymbals, to raise sounds of joy.

V.   When the song was raised in the praise of the Lord:
R.   The glory of the Lord filled the house of God.

Let us pray.   *(Silence)*

O God, whom saints and angels delight to worship in heaven, be ever present with your servants who seek through music to perfect the praises offered by your people on earth; and grant them even now glimpses of your beauty, and make them worthy at length to behold it unveiled for evermore; through Jesus Christ our Lord. *Amen.*

In the Name of God and of this congregation, I commission you [N.] as *Organist and Choirmaster* in this *Parish* [and give you this _____ as a token of your ministry].

9. Lectors

Sponsor   I present to you *these persons* to be admitted to the ministry of Lector in this congregation.

Antiphon

They read from the book, from the law of God, clearly; and they gave all the sense, so that the people understood the reading.

V. Your word is a lantern to my feet:
R. And a light upon my path.

Let us pray. *(Silence)*

Almighty God, whose blessed Son read the Holy Scriptures in the synagogue: Look graciously upon the lectors of your Church, and so enlighten them with wisdom and understanding that they may read your holy Word to the glory of your Name, and for the building up of your people; through Jesus Christ our Lord. *Amen.*

In the Name of God and of this congregation, I commission you [N.] as Lector in this *Parish* [and I give you this
_____as a token of your ministry].

10. Those Who Administer the Sacrament

Sponsor   I present to you *these persons* who *have* been chosen and licensed to administer the sacrament in this congregation.

Antiphon

The cup of blessing which we bless is a sharing in the Blood of Christ. The bread which we break is a sharing in the Body of Christ.

V. As often as you eat this bread and drink this cup:
R. You proclaim the Lord's death until he comes.

Let us pray. *(Silence)*

Grant, Almighty God, that those who minister the Bread of
Life and cup of blessing may live in love and holiness
according to your commandment, and at the last come to the
joy of your heavenly feast with all your saints in light;
through Jesus Christ our Lord. *Amen.*

In the Name of God and of this congregation, I commission
you [N.] to administer the sacrament in this *Parish* [and give
you this _____ as a token of your ministry].

11. Licensed Lay Readers

Sponsor   I present to you *this person* licensed by the Bishop
for the ministry of Lay Reader in this diocese.

Antiphon

There are varieties of gifts, but the same Spirit; and there are
varieties of service, but the same Lord; and there are
varieties of working, but it is the same God who inspires
them all in everyone.

V.   Let the word of Christ dwell in you richly:
R.   Do everything in the name of the Lord Jesus.

Let us pray   *(Silence)*

Look with favor upon those whom you have called, O Lord,
to be Lay Readers in your Church; and grant that they may
be so filled with your Holy Spirit that, seeking your glory
and the salvation of souls, they may minister your Word
with steadfast devotion, and by the constancy of their faith
and the innocency of their lives may adorn in all things the
doctrine of Christ our Savior; who lives and reigns for ever
and ever. *Amen.*

In the Name of God and of this congregation, I commission
you [N.] as Licensed Lay Reader [and give you this
_____ as a token of your ministry].

12. Parish Visitors

Sponsor   I present to you *these persons* to be admitted to the
ministry of Parish Visitor in this congregation.

Antiphon

Religion that is pure and undefiled before God and the
Father is this: to visit orphans and widows in their affliction
and to keep oneself unstained from the world.

V. Let not the needy, O Lord, be forgotten:
R. Nor the hope of the poor be taken away.

Let us pray. *(Silence)*

O God, your Son Jesus Christ said that we minister to him
when we clothe the naked, give food to the hungry and
drink to the thirsty, and visit the sick and imprisoned: Go
with all those who, following the command of your Christ,
visit your people in his Name; who lives and reigns for ever
and ever. *Amen.*

In the Name of God and of this congregation, I commission
you [N.] as Visitor in this *Parish* [and give you this
_____ as a token of your ministry].

13. Members of Prayer Groups

Sponsor   I present to you *these persons* who have accepted a
special ministry of intercessory prayer in this
congregation.

Antiphon

Rejoice always, pray constantly, give thanks in all circumstances; for this is the will of God in Christ Jesus for you.

V. In truth God has heard me:
R. He has attended to the voice of my prayer.

Let us pray. *(Silence)*

O God, whose Son our Lord on the night of his betrayal prayed for all his disciples: Hear the prayers of all those who accept the work and ministry of intercession on behalf of others, that the needs of many may be met and your will be done; through Jesus Christ our great High Priest. *Amen.*

[N.,] In the Name of God and of this congregation, I recognize your ministry of intercession in this *Parish* [and give you this _____ as a token of your ministry].

14. Parish Canvassers

Sponsor   I present to you *these persons* who have accepted the ministry of Canvasser in this congregation.

Antiphon

God, who supplies seed for sowing and bread for eating, will supply the seed you need, and produce a rich harvest.

V. Each one must do as he has made up his mind, not reluctantly or under compulsion:
R. For God loves a cheerful giver.

Let us pray. *(Silence)*

Lord Jesus Christ, you sent laborers to prepare for your coming: Be with all those who go forth in your Name, that by their witness and commitment the hearts of many will be turned to you; who live and reign for ever and ever. *Amen.*

In the Name of God and of this congregation, I commission you [N.] as Canvasser in this *Parish* [and give you this _____ as a token of your ministry].

15. Officers of Church Organizations

Sponsor   I present to you *these persons* to be installed as _____ of _____ in this congregation.

Antiphon

God will not overlook your work and the love which you show for his sake.

V.   Teach me to do what pleases you, for you are my God:
R.   Let your good Spirit lead me on level ground.

Let us pray. *(Silence)*

Regard, O Lord, our supplications, and confirm with your heavenly benediction your *servants* whom we admit today to the ministry (office) of _____; that with sincere devotion of mind and body *they* may offer you a service acceptable to your divine Majesty; through Jesus Christ our Lord. *Amen.*

In the Name of God and of this congregation, I admit you [N.] to the office of _____ of _____ [and give you this _____ as a token of your office].

16. Other Lay Ministries

Sponsor   I present to you *these persons* to be admitted to the ministry of _____ in this congregation.

The following, or some other antiphon, versicle and Collect may be used.

Antiphon

You are my witnesses, says the Lord, and my servants whom I have chosen.

V.   Give thanks to the Lord and call upon his Name:
R.   Make known his deeds among the peoples.

Let us pray. *(Silence)*

Have regard to our supplication, O gracious Lord, and confirm with your heavenly benediction your *servants* commissioned to minister in your Church, that with sincere devotion of mind and body *they* may offer acceptable service to you; through Jesus Christ our Lord. *Amen.*

In the Name of God and of this congregation, I commission you [N.] as _____ in this *Parish* [and give you this _____ as a token of your ministry].

When used with the Eucharist, the service continues with (the Prayers of the People and) the exchange of the Peace.

The following Collect may be used at the conclusion of the Prayers of the People

O Lord, without whom our labor is lost: We beseech you to prosper all works in your Church undertaken according to your holy will. Grant to your workers a pure intention, a patient faith, sufficient success on earth, and the blessedness of serving you in heaven; through Jesus Christ our Lord. *Amen.*

When used with the Daily Office, the service continues with the preceding prayer and the exchange of the Peace.

When used separately, it ends with the preceding prayer, the Lord's Prayer, the exchange of the Peace, and a blessing.

Scripture Readings

When used as a separate service, one of the following readings may be used at the discretion of the celebrant:

Numbers 11:16-17 (Gather for me seventy men of the elders of Israel.)
Deuteronomy 4:1-2,9 (Give heed to the statutes and ordinances which I teach you.)
1 Chronicles 9:26-30,32 (Some of them had charge of the utensils of service.)
Nehemiah 8:1-4a,5-6,8 (Ezra reads the Law of Moses to the people.)
Romans 12:6-12 (Having gifts that differ according to the grace given.)
2 Corinthians 4:2,5-6 (Having this ministry by the mercy of God.)
Colossians 3:12-17 (Sing psalms and hymns and spiritual songs.)
Hebrews 6:9-12 (God is not so unjust as to overlook your work and love.)
Matthew 5:14-16 (You are the light of the world.)
Mark 4:2-9 (A sower went forth to sow.)
Luke 12:35-37 (He will come and serve them.)
John 6:(1-7) 8-13 (There is a lad here who has five barley loaves.)

Dedication of Church Furnishings and Ornaments

In accordance with a venerable tradition, church furnishings and ornaments are consecrated by being put to the use for which they were intended. If a rite of dedication is desired, one of the following forms may be used after the sermon (and Creed) at the Eucharist, or at the Daily Office at the time of the hymn or anthem following the Collects

It is appropriate, when the object to be dedicated is fixed, that there be a procession to that place. If the procession is to a distant place, an anthem (the text of which may be the appointed antiphon), psalm, or hymn may be sung. When the object is portable, it should be brought to the Altar and presented to the celebrant.

The appointed antiphons may be read or sung by all, or by the celebrant, or by some other person.

If a longer form is desired, the presentation, versicles, and prayers on pages 212-213 may be used in connection with the proper form.

1. An Altar   *(Reserved to the Bishop)*

The dedication of an Altar takes place immediately before the Peace.

Antiphon

Arise, go to Bethel, and dwell there, and make there an altar to our God.

V. I will go to the altar of God:
R. To the God of my joy and gladness.

Let us pray.   *(Silence)*

The Bishop, standing at the Table with arms extended, says

We praise you, Almighty and eternal God, that for us and our salvation, you sent your Son Jesus Christ to be born among us, that through him we might become your sons and daughters.
Blessed be your Name, Lord God.

We praise you for his life on earth, and for his death upon the cross, through which he offered himself as a perfect sacrifice.
Blessed be your Name, Lord God.

We praise you for raising him from the dead, and for exalting him to be our great High Priest.
Blessed be your Name, Lord God.

We praise you for sending your Holy Spirit to make us holy, and to unite us in your holy Church.
Blessed be your Name, Lord God.

The Bishop lays a hand upon the Table, and continues

Lord God, hear us. Sanctify this Table dedicated to you. Let it be to us a sign of the heavenly Altar where your saints and angels praise you for ever. Accept here the continual recalling of the sacrifice of your Son. Grant that all who eat and drink at this holy Table may be fed and refreshed by his flesh and blood, be forgiven for their sins, united with one another, and strengthened for your service.
Blessed be your Name, Father, Son, and Holy Spirit; now and for endless ages. Amen.

Bells may then be rung and music played. If desired, the Bishop may cense the Altar. Members of the congregation then vest it, place the vessels on it, and light the candles. The Liturgy then continues with the Peace.

2. A Font   *(Reserved to the Bishop)*

It is desirable that the consecration of a Font take place at a service of public Baptism, in which case the following is inserted immediately before the Thanksgiving over the Water on page 306. Otherwise, it takes place as described on pages 196-197 of this book.

Antiphon

Repent and be baptized every one of you in the Name of Jesus Christ.

V.   All of us who are baptized into Christ:
R.   Have clothed ourselves with Christ.

Let us pray.   *(Silence)*

Father, we thank you that through the waters of Baptism we die to sin and are made new in Christ. Grant through your Spirit that those baptized here may enjoy the liberty and splendor of the children of God; through Jesus Christ our Lord. *Amen.*

We dedicate this Font in the Name of the Father, and of the Son, and of the Holy Spirit. *Amen.*

If desired, the Bishop may cense the Font.

When there are persons to be baptized, water is now poured into the Font, and the Bishop proceeds to the Thanksgiving over the Water.

If the consecration of the Font takes place apart from the service of Holy Baptism, (water may be poured into the Font and) the Bishop says

	The Lord be with you.
People	And also with you.
Bishop	Let us give thanks to the Lord our God.
People	It is right to give him thanks and praise.

We thank you, Almighty God, for the gift of water. Over it the Holy Spirit moved in the beginning of creation. Through it you led the children of Israel out of their bondage in Egypt into the land of promise. In it your Son Jesus received the baptism of John and was anointed by the Holy Spirit as the Messiah, the Christ, to lead us, through his death and resurrection, from the bondage of sin into everlasting life.

We thank you, Father, for the water of Baptism. In it we are buried with Christ in his death. By it we share in his resurrection. Through it we are reborn by the Holy Spirit. Therefore in joyful obedience to your Son, we bring into his fellowship those who come to him in faith, baptizing them in the Name of the Father, and of the Son, and of the Holy Spirit.

Grant, by the power of your Holy Spirit, that those who here are cleansed from sin and born again may continue for ever in the risen life of Jesus Christ our Savior.

To him, to you, and to the Holy Spirit, be all honor and glory, now and for ever. *Amen.*

3. Chalices and Patens   *(Traditionally reserved to the Bishop)*

Antiphon

Taste and see that the Lord is good; happy are they who trust in him.

V.   The cup of blessing which we bless is a sharing in the Blood of Christ.

R.   The bread which we break is a sharing in the Body of Christ.

Let us pray. *(Silence)*

Almighty God, whose blessed Son instituted the Sacrament
of his Body and Blood: Grant that all who receive the holy
Mysteries from *these vessels,* which we now consecrate for
use in your Church, may be sustained by his presence and
enjoy for ever his heavenly benediction; who lives and reigns
in glory everlasting. *Amen.*

4. A Bell   *(Traditionally reserved to the Bishop)*

Antiphon

Their sound has gone out into all lands, and their message to
the ends of the world.

V. I call to you, my people:
R. My voice is to the children of God.

Let us pray. *(Silence)*

O God, accept our offering of this bell, which we consecrate
today [and to which we give the name _____]: Grant
that in this generation and in those that are to come, its voice
may continually call your people to praise and worship;
through Jesus Christ our Lord. *Amen.*

5. A Cross

Antiphon

We will glory in the cross of our Lord Jesus Christ, in whom
is our salvation, our life and resurrection.

V. Christ for us became obedient unto death:
R. Even death on a cross.

Let us pray. *(Silence)*

O gracious God, who in your mercy ordained that your Son should suffer death on a cross of shame: We thank you that it has become for us the sign of his triumph and the banner of our salvation; and we pray that this cross may draw our hearts to him, who leads us to the glory of your kingdom; where you live and reign for ever and ever. *Amen.*

6. Candlesticks and Lamps

Antiphon

Before the throne burn seven lamps of fire, which are the seven spirits of God.

V. You, O Lord, are my lamp:
R. My God, you make my darkness bright.

Let us pray. *(Silence)*

O heavenly Father, who revealed to us the vision of your Son in the midst of the candlesticks, and of your Spirit in seven lamps of fire before your throne: Grant that *these lights* (*lamps*), to be kindled for your glory, may be to us a sign of your presence and the promise of eternal light; through Jesus Christ our Lord. *Amen.*

7. Altar Cloths and Hangings

Antiphon

This is the offering which you shall receive from the people gold, silver, and bronze, blue and purple and scarlet cloth, and finely woven linen.

V. O Lord my God, how excellent is your greatness:
R. You are clothed with majesty and splendor.

Let us pray. *(Silence)*

O glorious God, all your works proclaim your perfect beauty: Accept our offering of this _____, and grant that it may adorn this sanctuary and show forth your glory; through Jesus Christ our Lord. *Amen.*

8. A Service Book

Antiphon

Glorify the Lord, all you works of the Lord; praise him and highly exalt him for ever.

V. All kings shall bow down before him:
R. All nations shall do him service.

Let us pray. *(Silence)*

Bless us, O Lord of hosts, as we use this _____ which we dedicate to your service, and grant that as your saints and angels always serve you in heaven, so we may worship you acceptably on earth; through Jesus Christ our Lord. *Amen.*

9. A Bible, Lectionary, or Gospel Book

Antiphon

Whatever was written in former days was written for our instruction, that by steadfastness and by the encouragement of the Scriptures we might have hope.

V. Jesus opened their minds:
R. To understand the Scriptures.

Let us pray. *(Silence)*

O heavenly Father, whose blessed Son taught the disciples in all the Scriptures the things concerning himself: Accept this _____ which we dedicate here today, and grant that we may so diligently search your holy Word that we may find in it the wisdom that leads to salvation; through Jesus Christ our Lord. *Amen.*

10. A Repository for the Scriptures

Antiphon

When Moses finished writing down these laws in a book, he gave command to the Levites: Take this book and put it beside the ark of the covenant of the Lord your God.

V. Our hearts burned within us:
R. When Jesus opened to us the Scriptures.

Let us pray. *(Silence)*

Almighty God, who declared your will to the prophets and sages of Israel, and revealed your glory in the Word made flesh: Accept, we pray, this repository for the Holy Scriptures, and grant that through prayer and worship we may know you as you speak to us today; through Jesus Christ our Lord. *Amen.*

11. An Aumbry or Tabernacle for the Sacrament

Antiphon

Aaron shall set the bread before the Lord on a table of pure gold, on behalf of the people of Israel, as a covenant for ever.

V.   As often as you eat this bread and drink this cup:
R.   You proclaim the Lord's death until he comes.

Let us pray.   *(Silence)*

O Lord God, Father of our Savior Jesus Christ, who before his passion instituted the Sacrament of his Body and Blood: Grant that in this aumbry (tabernacle) which we set apart today, the outward signs of his covenant may be kept in safety, and that we may show forth his death and resurrection until he comes in glory; who lives and reigns for ever and ever. *Amen.*

12. An Aumbry for the Oils

Antiphon

The Israelites and Levites shall bring grain, new wine, and oil to the rooms where the vessels of the sanctuary are kept.

V.   You have anointed my head with oil:
R.   My cup is running over.

Let us pray.   *(Silence)*

O Lord God of hosts, who commanded priests of the Old Covenant to set apart oil for the anointing of kings and priests, and by your Apostle James commanded the presbyters of your Church to anoint the sick: We here offer to you this aumbry for the safe-keeping of the oils set apart for the anointing of baptism and for the ministry of healing; through him who was anointed as the Christ, and who lives and reigns for ever and ever. *Amen.*

13. An Ambo (Lectern-Pulpit)

Antiphon

Jesus, as his custom was, went into the synagogue on the Sabbath day and stood up to read.

V.   Your word is a lantern to our feet:
R.   And a light upon our path.

Let us pray.   *(Silence)*

Almighty God, in every age you have spoken through the voices of prophets, pastors, and teachers: Purify the lives and lips of those who read and proclaim your holy Word from this *ambo* which we dedicate today, that your word only may be proclaimed, and your word only may be heard; through Jesus Christ our Lord. *Amen.*

14. Chairs, Benches, and Prayer Desks

Antiphon

Round the heavenly throne were twenty-four other thrones, on which were seated twenty-four elders.

V.   The Lord has set his throne in heaven:
R.   And his kingship has dominion over all.

Let us pray. *(Silence)*

O Lord God Almighty, you disclosed in a vision the elders seated around your throne: Accept *this chair* for the use of those called to minister in your earthly sanctuary, and grant that those who serve you here may do so with reverence and love, to your honor and glory; through Jesus Christ our Lord. *Amen.*

15. A Stained Glass Window

Antiphon

I will make your windows of agates, and all your borders of pleasant stones.

V. Look upon the rainbow, and praise him who made it:
R. How beautiful it is in its brightness.

Let us pray. *(Silence)*

O Lord God, the whole world is filled with the radiance of your glory: Accept our offering of this window which we now dedicate to you for the adornment of this place and the inspiration of your people. Grant that as the light shines through it in many colors, so our lives may show forth the beauty of your manifold gifts of grace; through Jesus Christ our Lord. *Amen.*

16. Pictures and Statues

Antiphon

Christ is the icon of the invisible God; all things were created through him and for him.

V. The Word became flesh:
R. And dwelt among us.

Let us pray. *(Silence)*

Almighty God, whose Son our Savior manifested your glory in his flesh, and sanctified the outward and visible to be a means to perceive realities unseen: Accept, we pray, this representation of_____; and grant that as we look upon it, our hearts may be drawn to things which can be seen only by the eye of faith; through Jesus Christ our Lord. *Amen.*

17. An Organ or Other Musical Instrument

Antiphon

They sing to the tambourine and the lyre, and rejoice to the sound of the pipes.

V. Praise him with the sound of the trumpet:
R. Praise him with lyre and harp.

Let us pray. *(Silence)*

O Lord, before whose throne trumpets sound, and saints and angels sing the songs of Moses and the Lamb: Accept this *organ* for the worship of your temple, that with the voice of music we may proclaim your praise and tell it abroad; through Jesus Christ our Lord. *Amen.*

18. A Vessel for Incense

Antiphon

Another angel came and stood at the altar with a golden censer; he was given much incense, and the smoke of the incense rose with the prayers of the saints.

V. The four living creatures and the four and twenty elders fell down before the Lamb.
R. Each held golden vessels full of incense, which are the prayers of the saints.

Let us pray. *(Silence)*

Almighty God, whose only-begotten Son received from the wise men a gift of incense and made for us the pure oblation foretold by the prophet: We dedicate to your worship *this vessel*, that our prayers may ascend in your sight as the incense, and the pure oblation of our Lord be proclaimed from farthest east to farthest west; through Jesus Christ our Lord. *Amen.*

19. Surplices and Albs

Antiphon

A great multitude which no one could number, from every nation and tribe and people and tongue, stand before the throne and before the Lamb.

V. He has clothed me with garments of salvation:
R. He has covered me with the robe of righteousness.

Let us pray. *(Silence)*

O God, before whose heavenly throne your servants minister
to you, clothed in white robes: Accept *this* _____
which we dedicate for the use of the *ministers* of your
Church, that serving before your earthly throne, they may
worship you in spirit and in truth; through Jesus Christ our
Lord. *Amen.*

20. Vestments for the Liturgy

Antiphon

You shall make holy garments for Aaron, for glory and for
beauty.

V. Clothe your ministers with righteousness:
R. Let your people sing with joy.

Let us pray. *(Silence)*

O God, you revealed your Son clothed in majesty and glory:
Accept *this* _____ for the use of the *clergy* of your
Church, that, being clothed with humility as they minister to
you, they may show forth his eternal splendor; through Jesus
Christ our Lord. *Amen.*

21. A Funeral Pall

Antiphon

I will greatly rejoice in the Lord; my soul shall exult in my
God.

V. He has clothed me with the garments of salvation;
R. He has covered me with the robe of righteousness.

Let us pray. *(Silence)*

O God, who baptized us into the Body of your Son Jesus Christ, and made us members with different functions, all necessary and all to be honored: Make this pall a sign of our common membership in Christ, that we may know those who have departed this earthly life, not as the world esteems them, but as you know and love them; through Jesus Christ our Lord. *Amen.*

22. Any Church Ornament

Antiphon

Solomon beautified the sanctuary, and multiplied the vessels of the temple.

V.   Oh, the majesty and magnificence of God's presence!
R.   Oh, the power and the splendor of his sanctuary!

Let us pray. *(Silence)*

O God, whose blessed Son has sanctified and transfigured the use of material things: Receive *this* _____ which we offer, and grant that *it* may proclaim your love, benefit your Church, and minister grace and joy to those who use *it*; through Jesus Christ our Lord. *Amen.*

A Longer Form of Dedication

The longer form begins in the following manner.

The gift may be presented to the Celebrant with these words

I (We) present to you this _____ to be set apart for the service of Christ's holy Church.

The following versicles and prayer may be said

V. All things come from you, O Lord;
R. And from your own gifts do we give to you.
V. Prosper the work of our hands;
R. Prosper our handiwork.
V. Show your servants your works;
R. And your splendor to their children.

Let us pray.

Almighty God, we thank you that you have put it into the hearts of your people to make offerings for your service, and have been pleased to accept their gifts. Be with us now and bless us as we set apart *this* _____ to your praise and glory [and in memory (honor) of _____]; through Jesus Christ our Lord. *Amen.*

The proper form of dedication follows.

After the dedication, one or both of the following prayers may be said. Alternatively, the benefactors and persons to be commemorated may be remembered in the Prayers of the People.

In Commemoration

Almighty God, we remember before you today your faithful *servant N.(N.)*; and we pray that, having opened to *him* the gates of larger life, you will receive *him* more and more into your joyful service, that, with all who have faithfully served you in the past, *he* may share in the eternal victory of Jesus Christ our Lord. *Amen.*

For Benefactors

We bless your Name, O Lord, because it has pleased you to enable your *servant N.(N.)* to offer *this gift* for your worship. Remember *him* for good, and grant that all who benefit from *this gift* may show their thankfulness to you by using *it* in accordance with your will; through Jesus Christ our Lord. *Amen.*

The Founding of a Church

Ground Breaking

Before the service, four stakes are set in the ground, at the corners of the proposed building. Three cords are prepared, two to extend diagonally from corner to corner, a third to enclose the space. A spade is placed at the site of the Altar.

The bishop, or a priest appointed by the bishop, is the celebrant. Having vested nearby, the ministers, with the people, go in procession to the site of the building.

This Litany for the Church is sung or said during the procession.

God the Father, Creator of heaven and earth,
Have mercy on us.

God the Son, Redeemer of the world,
Have mercy on us.

God the Holy Spirit, Sanctifier of the faithful,
Have mercy on us.

Holy, blessed, and glorious Trinity, one God,
Have mercy on us.

O Christ the Rock, on which your people, as living stones joined together, grow into a spiritual house;
Defend your Church, we pray.

O Christ the Vine, of which your people are the branches;
Defend your Church, we pray.

O Christ the Head of the Body, of which your people are the members;
Defend your Church, we pray.

O Christ our Prophet, you teach the way of God in truth;
Defend your Church, we pray.

O Christ our Priest, you offered yourself upon the Cross, and now make intercession for us to the Father;
Defend your Church, we pray.

O Christ our King, you reign over all the earth, and make us citizens of your heavenly kingdom;
Defend your Church, we pray.

O Christ, you sent the Holy Spirit upon the Church, clothing it with power from on high;
Defend your Church, we pray.

We pray to you, Lord Christ.
Lord, hear our prayer.

That we may be devoted to the Apostles' teaching and fellowship, to the breaking of bread and the prayers,
Lord, hear our prayer.

That we may make disciples of all nations, baptizing them in the Name of the Father, and of the Son, and of the Holy Spirit,
Lord, hear our prayer.

That you will fulfill your promise to be with us always, even to the ages of ages,
Lord, hear our prayer.

That you will sustain all members of your holy Church, that in our vocation and ministry we may truly and devoutly serve you,
Lord, hear our prayer.

That you will bless the clergy of your Church, that they may diligently preach the Gospel and faithfully celebrate the holy Sacraments,
Lord, hear our prayer.

That you will heal the divisions in your Church, that all may be one, even as you and the Father are one,
Lord, hear our prayer.

Arise, O God, maintain your cause;
Do not forget the lives of the poor.

Look down from heaven, behold and tend this vine;
Preserve what your right hand has planted.

Let your priests be clothed with righteousness;
Let your faithful people sing with joy.

The Celebrant says

	The Lord be with you.
People	And also with you.
Celebrant	Let us pray.

Let your continual mercy cleanse and defend your Church, O Lord; and, because it cannot continue in safety without your help, protect and govern it always by your goodness; through Jesus Christ our Lord, who lives and reigns with you and the Holy Spirit, one God, for ever and ever. *Amen.*

Glory to God whose power, working in us, can do infinitely more than we ask or imagine: Glory to him from generation to generation in the Church, and in Christ Jesus for ever and ever. *Amen.*

A hymn may be sung.

Then a Person appointed reads

Genesis 28:10-17

A sermon or address may follow.

While the following antiphon and psalm are being sung, persons appointed stretch two cords diagonally across the space, from the northeast to the southwest, and from the southeast to the northwest, securing them to the stakes, thus forming the Greek letter X (chi), the symbol both of the cross and of the name of Christ.

Antiphon (to be used before and after the Psalm)

Let us go to God's dwelling place; let us fall upon our knees before his footstool.

Psalm 132:1-9(10-19)

During the following antiphon and psalm, persons appointed stretch the third cord completely around the four stakes, enclosing the area. They move clockwise, beginning and ending at the southeast corner.

The ministers and people may follow in procession.

Antiphon

How wonderful is God in his holy places! the God of Israel, giving strength and power to his people! Blessed be God!

Psalm 48:1-3,7-13

Then the Celebrant, standing at the site of the Altar, says

Since faithful people desire to build a house of prayer,
dedicated to the glory of God [and in honor of _____]
[to be known as _____], on this ground, now marked
with the symbol of Christ;

*Then, taking the spade, and breaking the ground, the Celebrant
continues*

Therefore, I break ground for this building, in the Name of
the Father, and of the Son, and of the Holy Spirit.

May the Gospel be preached,
the Sacraments administered,
and prayers and praises offered in this place,
from generation to generation. *Amen.*

The Celebrant then says

	The Lord be with you.
People	And also with you.
Celebrant	Let us pray.

People and Celebrant

Our Father, who art in heaven,	Our Father in heaven,
hallowed be thy Name,	hallowed be your Name,
thy kingdom come,	your kingdom come,
thy will be done,	your will be done
on earth as it is in heaven.	on earth as in heaven.
Give us this day our daily bread.	Give us today our daily brea
And forgive us our trespasses,	Forgive us our sins
as we forgive those	as we forgive those
who trespass against us.	who sin against us.
And lead us not into temptation,	Save us from the time of tria
but deliver us from evil.	and deliver us from evil.
For thine is the kingdom,	For the kingdom, the power
and the power, and the glory,	and the glory are yours,
for ever and ever. Amen.	now and for ever. Amen.

V. How wonderful is God in his holy places!
R. Establish, O God, what you have wrought for us.
V. Be favorable and gracious to Zion:
R. Build up the walls of Jerusalem.

Celebrant   Let us pray.

O Lord God of Israel, the heavens cannot contain you, yet
you are pleased to dwell in the midst of your people, and
have moved us to set apart a space on which to build a house
of prayer: Accept and bless the work which we have now
begun, that it may be brought to completion, to the honor
and glory of your holy Name; through Jesus Christ our
Lord, who lives and reigns with you in the unity of the Holy
Spirit, one God, for ever and ever. *Amen.*

A Deacon or the Celebrant then dismisses the people.

Laying of a Cornerstone

*If the laying of a cornerstone takes place before the building is erected,
the following order may be observed.*

1. A hymn or anthem is sung.

2. A suitable passage of Scripture, such as Ephesians 2:19-22, may be
   read.

3. An address follows.

4. An appropriate prayer, such as the Collect of the Patron or Title of
   the Church, is said.

5. The cornerstone is then laid, after which the Celebrant prays as
   follows

Let us pray.

Lord Jesus Christ, Son of the living God, you are the brightness of the Father's glory and the express image of his person, the one foundation and the chief cornerstone: Bless what we have now done in the laying of this stone. Be the beginning, the increase, and the consummation of this work undertaken to the glory of your Name; who with the Father and the Holy Spirit live and reign, one God, for ever and ever. *Amen.*

Trumpets may be sounded, and the Celebrant says

Praise the Lord, because the foundation of the house of the Lord is laid!

The People respond, with a loud voice

Alleluia! Alleluia! Alleluia!

Applause may follow.

6. A hymn is sung, after which the rite is concluded with a blessing and dismissal.

If the laying of a cornerstone takes place after the building is completed, it is suitable that it take place in the context of a celebration of the Holy Eucharist. After the homily, a hymn, psalm, or anthem is sung, during which all go in procession to the site of the ceremony. An appropriate prayer (such as the Collect of the Patron or Title of the Church) is said, after which the cornerstone is laid. The rite then continues with the Celebrant's prayer given above. During the hymn that follows, the procession returns to the church where the Liturgy continues with (the Creed and) the Prayers of the People.

Concerning the Service

This service has been created to help congregations and dioceses who are considering a new church mission, to discern the will of the Holy Spirit. The service may also be used by a team preparing for a new church plant, and/or be incorporated into one or several Sunday services by supporting/sponsoring congregation(s). The service may be used to initiate a period of intentional discernment; and at points within that process.

The service encourages silence and stillness to listen to the movement of the Holy Spirit. It is not a Eucharistic liturgy.

It is appropriate to adapt this rite to local custom, language, dialect, and idiom.

Discernment for a New Church Mission

Officiant   Be still before the Lord,
People   And wait patiently for God's presence.

A period of silence is kept.

Officiant   O Holy Spirit, you are the seeker's resource and guide.
People   Come, create, renew and inspire.
Officiant   Teach us to hear, teach us to speak.
People   Show us your will that we may follow.

One or two Lessons are read.
A list of suggested lessons and psalms

I Kings 3:3-10 (The Lord asks Solomon, "Ask what I shall give you.")
Isaiah 49: 5-13 (I will give you as a light to the nations, that my salvation may reach...)
Ruth 1: 8-18. (Your people shall be my people, and your God my God...)
Hosea 6:1-6, 11-7:1a (For you also, O Judah, a harvest is appointed)

Psalms: 37, 46

Matthew 28:17-20 (Go therefore and make disciples of all nations...)
John 5:25-39 (I seek not my own will but the will of him who sent me.)
Ephesians 1:1-14 (For he has made known to us ... the mystery of his will)

A significant period of silence is kept after each Scripture Reading. A sermon or homily is discouraged in favor of time to listen to the movement of the Holy Spirit.

After the [second] period of silence, a person appointed leads the Litany, page 246.

Litany for the Mission of the Church

The Officiant then continues with one of the following, or some other suitable Collect.

A Collect for Parish-led Church Planting

O God, who inspired your apostles in Jerusalem to pray and fast to discern your will: Send us your Spirit, that we may learn what you would have us do and the words and witness you would have us offer, that your Kingdom may come and your power be revealed in this *(diocese, deanery, town)*; to the glory of your Name. *Amen.*

A Collect for Apostolic-model Church Planting

Gracious Father, you sent your Son Jesus to proclaim to all the Good News of your Kingdom, and through him inspired individuals to sow the seeds of your Church: Guide us as we continue this work; show us the next field in which to plant; and give us the gifts to accomplish your will; all of which we ask through Jesus our Savior. *Amen.*

A Collect for Regional Collaboration in Church Planting

O Holy God, you breathe your life-giving Spirit into the congregations of this *(region, deanery, ...)*, calling us to join together in mission for the spreading of the Gospel: Show us the people to whom we should go and the path we should travel; help us to understand the deep longings of their hearts, and enable us to feed them through the living presence of Jesus Christ our Savior, in whose power we set forth and in whose Name we pray. *Amen.*

A Collect for Multicultural Church Planting

Eternal God, you have promised your salvation to all peoples, and have given us a vision of a great multitude around your throne, from all nations and tribes and languages: Help us to bring this vision into our time and place; banish from us all prejudices and false presumptions; and enable us to hear and to speak new words of hope and praise; through Jesus Christ, the living Word. *Amen.*

A Collect for Regular Use during Sunday Worship by Congregations in Discernment

Lord Jesus, you commissioned us to make disciples of all the nations and promised that you would be with us always: So guide this congregation to see the peoples you would have us reach and empower us to be instruments of your saving work, for the glory of God. *Amen.*

or

Blessed God, you make all things new: Guide us as we seek your will for a new community of Word and Sacrament, that it may be leaven for the world's bread, and wine of delight for hearts in need; a gathering strong for service and glad in praise; and a people listening and responding to your presence in their midst; through Jesus our Redeemer and steadfast companion. *Amen.*

A Collect for Raising Up of People with Skills Needed for a Church Planting

Holy Spirit, you delight to equip us with all the gifts of service *(especially ___)* to extend the Realm of God: Raise up among us and empower those among us whom you call to this new work, that the Body of Christ may grow in strength and health, for the transforming of the world; through Jesus Christ our Lord. *Amen.*

The Lord's Prayer

The Officiant introduces the prayer with this or some other sentence.

Gathering our prayers into one, as Jesus taught us we now pray:

Our Father...

A deacon, or the Officiant, dismisses the people using the following or some other suitable dismissal

Go forth now in the Name of Christ.
Go into the (*City, town, village, region...*) of _____.
Go into your own neighborhoods.
Go to unknown lands and places.
Go where God's name is well known and where it has yet to be known.
Go to those who welcome you and to those who reject you.
Go forth into the world and share the Good News of God's love. [Alleluia, Alleluia!]

The People respond   Thanks be to God. [Alleluia, Alleluia!]

In Lent the Alleluias are omitted. In Easter season they are included.

Concerning the Service

This liturgy is designed for use on the occasion when a selected and trained church planter, missioner and/or mission team is to be sent forth by a diocese (and sponsoring congregation), to a designated location/congregation. If the new church has been named, there are opportunities in the liturgy for that designation. The service should be adapted to the mission circumstances.

This is a Eucharistic liturgy. It presumes the participation of the diocesan bishop or bishop's representative; clergy and other members of any sponsoring congregation(s); and the church planter and his/her team, their supporters, and members of the new church.

The liturgy is rooted in the imagery and theology of Baptism, recognizing that the work of spreading the Gospel and building up of Christ's Body the Church is the work of all baptized persons. With that understanding, particular ministers are commissioned and their responsibilities recognized in this liturgy.

It is appropriate to adapt this rite to local custom, language, dialect, and idiom.

A Liturgy for Commissioning a Church Planter, Missioner or Mission Team

A hymn or anthem may be sung.

An Opening Acclamation from the Book of Common Prayer (page 299) or Enriching our Worship I (page 50) is used

Then follows

Celebrant	There is one Body and one Spirit;
People	There is one hope in God's call to us;
Celebrant	One Lord, one Faith, one Baptism;
People	One God and Father of all.

A song of praise may be sung.

Celebrant	The Lord be with you.
People	And also with you.
Celebrant	Let us pray.

One of the following collects; or the Collect of the Day; or one of the collects for the Mission of the Church (BCP pages 257, 816) follows.

For Parish-led Church Planting

Lord Christ, you equipped and sent forth your friends to bring the Good News of salvation from Jerusalem into Judea and all the world: Be present as we send forth these friends and companions in your service, that your Kingdom may come with power in ____ [*place or name of new church*]; to the glory of your Name. *Amen.*

For Apostolic-model Church Planting

Gracious God, you sent your Son Jesus to proclaim to all
the Good News of your Kingdom, and through him inspired
individuals to sow the seeds of your Church: Help us as we
continue this work. Empower *N.* your servant and all who
support *her*, and give them the gifts to accomplish your will;
all of which we ask through Jesus our Savior. *Amen.*

For Regional Collaboration in Church Planting

O Holy God, you breathe your life-giving Spirit into the
congregations of this (*region, deanery, ...*), calling us to join
together in mission for the spreading of the Gospel: Bless
us as we begin this new journey; go with those whom you
have raised up for this work; and enable them to feed your
people in _____ through the living presence of Jesus Christ our
Savior, in whose power we set forth and in whose Name we
pray. *Amen.*

A Collect for Multicultural Church Planting

Eternal God, you have promised your salvation to all
peoples, and have given us a vision of a great multitude
around your throne, from all nations and tribes and
languages: Help us as we bring this vision into our time and
place; go with those who now undertake your work in _____;
and enable them to hear and to speak new words of hope
and praise; through Jesus Christ, the living Word. *Amen.*

For Any Church Planters

O Holy God, you raise up laborers for your harvest, sending
them out as sowers of your Gospel and caretakers of new

life: Bless *these your servants* in *their* work of planting and tending your Church in ____; equip *them* for service, enliven *them* with your joy, and help *them* remember and trust that it is you who will bring in the harvest; through Jesus Christ, the Savior of souls. *Amen.*

or

Blessed God, you call forth light from darkness: Send the power of your Spirit upon your servants N. *(and N.)* as *they* carry your Gospel to _____. May your light so fill *them* that *they* may shine with your radiance, drawing all to the brightness of your love and mercy; through Jesus, our Savior and true Light. *Amen.*

Then one or more of the following passages from Holy Scripture is read. Other passages particularly suited to the day may be substituted. If there is to be a Communion, a passage from the Gospel always concludes the readings.

Joshua 1:6-9 *(call of Joshua)*
Isaiah 6: 1-8 *(call of Isaiah)*
Jeremiah: 1:5-10 *(call of Jeremiah)*

Psalms: 65, 66; 100; 115; 147

Acts: 13:1-4 *(setting apart for church planting of Paul and Barnabas)*
Acts 16:6-10 *(the call of Paul to Macedonia)*
Acts: 18:1-4, 7-10 *(Paul's vision of Christ in Corinth: "I have many people in this city")*
Romans 15:13-21 *(May the God of hope fill you with all joy...)*
I Corinthians 3:5-12 *(Paul plants, Apollos watered, and God gives the increase)*
II Corinthians 5:16-6:2 *(We are ambassadors for Christ)*
Ephesians 2:13-22 *(He preached peace to those who were far off...)*

A hymn, psalm or anthem may be sung.

Matthew 9: 36-38 *(Jesus has compassion on the people)*
Matthew 28:16-20 *(Go, make disciples of all nations, baptizing them...)*
Luke 10:1-9 *(Pray the Lord of the harvest to send laborers)*
Luke 24:44-50 *(Forgiveness of sins will be preached to all peoples)*
John 4:34-38 *(Look at the fields, they are white with harvest)*

The Sermon

The Commissioning

The church planter/team stands before the bishop or the bishop's representative and representatives of the diocese, sponsoring congregation(s), and others as appropriate. If there are members of the new congregation already identified, they should stand with the planting team

The Bishop or the Bishop's Representative says

> The *vicar (missioner, team...)* and members of the new congregation ____ will now be presented.

The rector of the sending parish, or a diocesan representative, says

> I present N. to be commissioned as a *church planter*, and to serve as *vicar* of ____ in the Diocese of ____.

The Bishop says

> Do you believe that *she* is well qualified and duly prepared for this ministry?

The Rector or Diocesan Representative responds   I do.

Bishop   N., do you, in the presence of this congregation, commit yourself to this new trust and responsibility?

Planter   I do.

Planter   I present these persons who represent all those who will serve with me in planting this new church.

Bishop   Will you who are committing yourselves to this new work do all in your power to support the life and mission of this new congregation?

Members of the team and/or new congregation   We will.

The Bishop then addresses the whole assembly

Will you who witness this new beginning, support and uphold N. *(these persons)* and the community of ____ in this ministry?

People   We will.

Appropriate symbols of the new ministry may be given.

Bishop   Let us join with those who are accepting this ministry of the Gospel, and renew our own baptismal covenant.

The Baptismal Covenant

Bishop   Do you believe in God the Father?
People   I believe in God, the Father almighty,
                creator of heaven and earth.
Bishop   Do you believe in Jesus Christ, the Son of God?
People   I believe in Jesus Christ, his only Son, our Lord.
                He was conceived by the power of the Holy Spirit
                    and born of the Virgin Mary.
                He suffered under Pontius Pilate,
                    was crucified, died, and was buried.
                He descended to the dead.
                On the third day he rose again.

He ascended into heaven,
and is seated at the right hand of the Father.
He will come again to judge the living and the dead.

Bishop Do you believe in God the Holy Spirit?
People I believe in the Holy Spirit,
the holy catholic Church,
the communion of saints,
the forgiveness of sins,
the resurrection of the body,
and the life everlasting.

Bishop Will you continue in the apostles' teaching and
fellowship, in the breaking of bread, and in the
prayers?
People I will, with God's help.

Bishop Will you persevere in resisting evil, and, whenever
you fall into sin, repent and return to the Lord?
People I will, with God's help.

Bishop Will you proclaim by word and example the Good
News of God in Christ?
People I will, with God's help.

Bishop Will you seek and serve Christ in all persons, loving
your neighbor as yourself?
People I will, with God's help.

Bishop Will you strive for justice and peace among all
people, and respect the dignity of every human
being?
People I will, with God's help.

Bishop Let us offer our prayers to God for all people and for this new congregation.

The Litany for the Mission of the Church (page 246) or the following Litany of Thanksgiving is led by a person appointed.

For the Church universal, of which you, O Christ, are the foundation and chief cornerstone,
We thank you, Lord.

For your presence whenever two or three have gathered together in your Name,
We thank you, Lord.

For making us your children by adoption and grace, and refreshing us day by day with the bread of life,
We thank you, Lord.

For the knowledge of your will and the grace to perform it,
We thank you, Lord.

For the fulfilling of our desires and petitions as may be best for us,
We thank you, Lord.

For the pardoning of our sins, which restores us to the company of your faithful people,
We thank you, Lord.

For the blessing of lives with your goodness,
We thank you, Lord.

For the faith and perseverance of those who have gone
before us,
We thank you, Lord.

For the fellowship of (Mary the God-bearer, the holy apostles,
blessed N. and of) all the saints,
We thank you, Lord.

After a period of silent prayer, the Bishop concludes with the following

O God, we praise you for the redemption of the world
through the death and resurrection of Jesus the Christ. We
thank you for pouring out your Spirit upon us, making some
apostles, some prophets, some evangelists, some pastors and
teachers to equip your people for the building up of the Body
of Christ. Bless this new work that we undertake, that your
Name may be glorified, now and for ever. *Amen.*

The Peace

The Eucharist continues with the Great Thanksgiving, the Bishop or Bishop's representative, or Rector of the sending parish, presiding at the table and the planters assisting according to their order.

Except for major feasts, the Preface is that of Pentecost.

In place of the usual postcommunion prayer, the following may be said

Celebrant or other person appointed

Eternal Giver of love and life, you have nourished us with the Body and Blood of your Son Jesus Christ. Now send us into the world to preach your Good News, to do your justice, and to walk humbly in your way.

People

Glory to God, whose power working in us can do infinitely more than we can ask or imagine. Glory to God from generation to generation in the Church, and in Christ Jesus for ever and ever. Amen.

The Bishop or Celebrant may bless the people.

The following or another form of the Dismissal is used

Deacon or Celebrant	Go forth into the world, sharing the Good News of God's love. [Alleluia, alleluia.]
People	We go in the Name of Christ. [Alleluia, alleluia.]

The alleluias are omitted in Lent. They are used in the Easter Season.

Concerning the Service

The opening service of a new congregation is a celebration for the members of the new community, but more importantly, an opportunity for them to show hospitality to those seeking a church home in the broader community.

It is important to choose a day appropriate for the culture surrounding the new mission–for example, the feast of the Epiphany is of particular significance in the Hispanic community and an effective date for a public launch. Days such as Palm Sunday, Easter, and Christmas are not recommended. Experience shows that dates between late August through the Last Sunday after Pentecost work well in most contexts.

The congregation is gathered to serve those coming for the first time, and should be mindful of the opportunities to proclaim the Gospel within the liturgy. The host members should be conscientious of the need for simplicity and clarity. It is important that a variety of persons participate in the leadership of the service.

This service assumes a Eucharistic context. It may be adapted to a service of the Word.

If appropriate the Liturgy for Setting Apart Secular Space for Sacred Use (page 245) may immediately precede the service.

It is appropriate to adapt this rite to local custom, language, dialect, and idiom.

A Liturgy for the Opening of a New Congregation

The Gathering

One of the following, or an Opening Acclamation from the Book of Common Prayer (page 355) or Enriching Our Worship I (page 50), may be used

Officiant/Celebrant	Holy God, you have called for yourself a people.
People	Fill us with your presence, affirm us with your love.

or

Officiant/Celebrant	This is the day that the Lord has made.
People	Let us rejoice and be glad in it.

Opening Prayer *The following or the Collect of the Day may be used.*

Officiant/Celebrant	O God, the source of all beginnings: we thank you for bringing us to this new day.
People	Send us your Spirit as we begin our journey as the people of _____ [name of congregation]. Equip us to proclaim the Good News of Jesus, defend us from all evil, and give us the grace to live together in peace and common prayer. In your power, may we become a holy community that transforms the world around us.

| *Officiant/Celebrant* | All this we ask through Jesus Christ our Savior, who lives and reigns with you and the Holy Spirit, one God, for ever and ever. *Amen.* |

The Word

The Proper of the Day, or two or more of the following may be used.

From the Old Testament
Exodus 6:2-8 (I will take you as my people)
Ezekiel 11:17-20 (I will gather you from the peoples)
Ezekiel 36:23b-30 (The nations shall know that I am the Lord)

Between the readings, a Psalm, hymn, or canticle may be sung or said. Appropriate Psalms are 67 and 98.

From the New Testament

2 Corinthians 5:16-21 (So if anyone is in Christ, there is a new creation)
Hebrews 10:19-25 (Let us hold fast to the confession of our hope)

The Gospel

John 13:31-35 (As I have loved you, you also should love one another)
Matthew 11:2-6 (the blind receive their sight, the lame walk)

A sermon, homily or other reflection follows the readings.

Prayers of the People

Here prayers are offered, which may include

A Litany for the Mission of the Church *(page 246)*
Prayers of the People *(such as BCP pages 383-393)*
General Intercessions and Thanksgivings

At the Eucharist

Preface *The Preface for Pentecost, for Apostles and Ordinations or another preface appropriate to the occasion is used.*

Post-Communion Prayers *Prayers especially appropriate are prayers found on pages 229 and 230 of the Commissioning liturgy; in Enriching Our Worship I, page 69; in the BCP, page 366*

Dismissal

Officiant/Celebrant   Let us go forth into the world, rejoicing in the power of the Spirit. [Alleluia, alleluia.]

People   Thanks be to God. [Alleluia, alleluia.]

In Lent, the alleluias are omitted. In the Easter Season, they are included.

Concerning the Service

This rite is designed for use by a church planting team or new congregation, as it begins worship in a facility such as a school, nursing home, "storefront" or other secular space. With adaptation it could be used in a variety of other situations, such as the initial gathering of a retreat group in a hotel. It anticipates regular but not exclusive use of the room or building for worship purposes. It may be desirable to place in the room significant symbols of Christian worship, such as a cross, candles, banner, etc., before or during the service.

An Entrance Hymn may be sung, and the congregation and liturgical ministers may process to the site of dedication, if appropriate. A large cross may be placed in a location visible to all.

It is appropriate to adapt this rite to local custom, language, dialect, and idiom.

Setting Apart Secular Space for Sacred Use

Antiphon

You will bring them in and plant them, O Lord,
in the sanctuary you have established.

V.   All your works praise you, O God,
R.   And your faithful servants bless you.

or (especially if a cross has just been put in place)

V.   Through the Cross of Jesus,
R.   We have been brought near and reconciled to God.

Officiant   Let us pray.

Blessed are you, O God, ruler of the universe. Your gifts are many, and in wisdom you have made all things to give you glory. Be with us now and bless us as we dedicate our use of this *space* to your praise and honor. As often as we worship you here, precede us and abide with us. Be known to us in the Word spoken and heard, in fellowship with one another, and in the breaking of bread. Give us joy in all your works, and grant that this *space* may be a place where your will is done and your name is glorified; through Jesus Christ our Savior, in the power of the Holy Spirit, we pray. *Amen.*

At a celebration of the Eucharist the Gloria in Excelsis *or other Song of Praise may be sung, as all take their places for worship. The Collect of the Day or Collect for an Opening Liturgy would follow. At a service of Morning/Evening Prayer or similar, an appropriate Invitatory psalm or hymn may follow the dedication.*

A Litany for the Mission of the Church

Holy God, in whom all things in heaven and earth have
their being,
Have mercy on us.

Jesus the Christ, through whom the world is reconciled to
the Father,
Have mercy on us.

Holy Spirit, whose glory fills the world and searches the
depths of God,
Have mercy on us.

Blessed Trinity, source of both unity and diversity,
Have mercy on us.

From blind hearts and petty spirits, that refuse to see the
need of all humankind for your love,
Savior, deliver us.

From pride, self-sufficiency and the unwillingness to
admit our own need of your compassion,
Savior, deliver us.

From discouragement in the face of pain and
disappointment, and from lack of persistence and
thoroughness,
Savior, deliver us.

From ignorance, apathy, and complacency that prevent us
from spreading the Gospel,
Savior, deliver us.

O God, we pray for the gifts of ministry.
Inspire our minds with a vision of your kingdom in this time
and place.
Hear us, O Christ.

Touch our eyes, that we may see your glory in all creation.
Hear us, O Christ.

Touch our ears, that we may hear from every mouth the
hunger for hope and stories of refreshment.
Hear us, O Christ.

Touch our lips, that we may tell in every tongue and dialect
the wonderful works of God.
Hear us, O Christ.

Touch our hearts, that we may discern the mission to which
you call us.
Hear us, O Christ.

Touch our feet, that we may take your Good News into our
neighborhoods, communities, and all parts of the world.
Hear us, O Christ.

Touch our hands, that we may each accomplish the work you
give us to do.
Hear us, O Christ.

Strengthen and encourage all who minister in your name in lonely, dangerous and unresponsive places.
Hear us, O Christ.

Open the hearts and hands of many to support your Church in this and every place.
Hear us, O Christ.

The Litany concludes with a collect, such as those provided in the Church Planting Liturgies or a collect for the Mission of the Church (BCP pages 257, 816).

A variety of Church Planting collects, blessings and other prayers

These collects may be used and adapted for a variety of situations, such as sending forth church planters, evangelists, missioners, stewardship committee members, etc.

O God the Creator and ruler of all things, your reign grows like a mustard seed into abundant life: Bless those who plant and tend the new life of your Church, that it may become a place of welcome, a refuge of healing, a school for souls, and a life-giving spring; all of which we ask through Jesus Christ, our strength and our salvation. *Amen.*

Blessed God, who makes all things new: Grant that this young community of Word and Sacrament may be leaven for the world's bread, and wine of delight for hearts in need; a gathering strong for service and glad in praise; and a people listening and responding to your presence in their midst; through Jesus our redeemer and steadfast companion. *Amen.*

You raise up laborers for your harvest, Holy God, sending them out as sowers of your good news, workers of healing, and caretakers of new life: Bless N. *(and N.)* in *their* work of planting and tending your Church *(in ____)*; equip *them* for service, enliven *them* with your joy, and help *them* remember and trust that it is you who will bring in the harvest; through Jesus Christ, the Savior of souls. *Amen.*

Blessed God, you call forth light from darkness: Send the power of your Spirit upon your servants N. *(and N.)*as *they* carry your Gospel to _____. May your light so fill *them* that *they* may shine with your radiance, drawing all to the brightness of your love and mercy; through Jesus, our Savior and true Light. *Amen.*

Jesus, Savior, made known to us in broken bread and in wine poured out for reconciliation: Give us good courage for this work of mission that as we, too, are broken, poured, and shared for the world's feeding, we find ourselves made whole in you. *Amen.*

Most Holy and life-giving God the friends of Jesus carried your good news, each to a different place according to their gifts and calling. Bless N. (and N.) as they carry your word of love, making disciples for your service and building up your Church; through the power of your Spirit and in the Name of Jesus. *Amen.*

A prayer of dedication

Christ Jesus, you go before and behind *us/me*, you are *our* light and *our* shield; guide *our* path, be *our* clear sight, lift *us* up in your Gospel joy, and bless the work *we* do in your name and honor, for you are *our* beloved, and *our* life made new. *Amen.*

Hymn suggestions for Church Planting liturgies

From *The Hymnal 1982*

302/303 Father, we thank thee who hast planted
304 I come with joy to meet my Lord
521 Put forth, O God, thy Spirit's might
527 Singing songs of expectation
528 Lord, you give the great commission (Rowthorn)
530 Spread, O spread thou mighty Word
537 Christ for the world we sing!
576/577 God is love, and where true love is

From *Wonder, Love, and Praise*

741 Filled with the Spirit's power
752 There's a sweet, sweet Spirit
761 All who hunger gather gladly
763 As we gather at your table
778 We all are one in mission
779 The church of Christ in every age
780 Lord, you give the great commission (Abbot's Leigh)
782 Gracious Spirit, give your servants
787 We are marching in the light of God
794 Muchos resplandores
796 Unidos
811 You shall cross the barren desert
812 I, the Lord of sea and sky
819 Guide my feet Lord

From *Lift Every Voice and Sing II*

50 The angel said to Philip
120 There's a sweet, sweet Spirit in this place
159 How to reach the masses
160 This little light of mine
161 "Go preach my gospel," saith the Lord

De *El Himnario*

2 Es tiempo de que alabemos a Dios
9 Todo se hace para la gloria de Dios
14 Grandes y maravillosas son tus obras
19 Señor, ¿qué es nuestro templo?
33 Cantemos al amor de los amores
56 Hay un dulce espíritu
205 Iglesia de Cristo, tu santa misión
209 Es Cristo de su Iglesia
213 ¡Suelta la alegría!
216 Muchos resplandores
223 Somos uno en espíritu
243 Una espiga
246 Te ofrecemos, Padre nuestro
252 Somos pueblo que camina
303 He decidido seguir a Cristo
306 Yo, el Dios de cielo y mar
312 A este santo templo
313 Tú has venido a la orilla (también en WLP 758)
317 Caminenos a la luz de Dios
321 Dios hoy nos llama
322 Sois la semilla
324 Yo soy sal de mi tierra

Lo Concerniente al Rito

Este rito se ha preparado para ayudar a las congregaciones y diócesis que están considerando fundar una iglesia o una misión nueva, a discernir la voluntad del Espíritu Santo. El rito lo puede usar el grupo que se prepara para fundar una iglesia. También puede ser incorporado en uno o varios ritos de la(s) congregación(es) que apoya(n) o patrocina(n) la misión. El rito se puede usar para iniciar un período de discernimiento y en otras oportunidades durante ese proceso.

El rito invita al silencio y a la calma para sentir el movimiento del Espíritu Santo. No es una liturgia eucarística.

Es apropiado adaptar estos ritos a constumbres locales de dialecto e idioma.

Discernimiento sobre la fundación de una iglesia-misión nueva

Oficiante	Estén tranquilos ante el Señor,
Pueblo	Y esperen pacientemente la presencia de Dios.

Se guarda un periodo de silencio.

Oficiante que busca.	Oh Santo Espíritu, que eres recurso y guía del
Pueblo	Ven, crea, renueva e inspira.
Oficiante	Enséñanos a escuchar, enséñanos a hablar.
Pueblo	Muéstranos tu voluntad para que la sigamos.

Se leen una o dos lecturas.
He aquí una lista de lecturas y salmos:

1 Reyes 3:3-10 (El Señor dijo a Salomón: Pídeme lo que quieras que te de.)
Isaías 49:5-13 (Te voy a poner por luz de las gentes, para que mi salvación alcance...)
Rut 1:8-19 (Tu pueblo será mi pueblo y tu Dios mi Dios...)
Oseas 6:1-6, 11-7:1a (También para ti, Judá, hay preparada una cosecha)

Salmos: 37, 46

Mateo 28:17-20 (Id, haced discípulos a todas las gentes, bautizándolas...)
Juan 5:25-39 (No busco mi voluntad sino la del que me ha enviado)
Efesios 1:1-14 (Porque nos ha dado a conocer... el misterio de su voluntad)

Se guarda un significativo período de silencio después de cada lectura. No se aconseja sermón ni homilía para que en el silencio se pueda sentir el movimiento del Espíritu Santo.

Después del [segundo] período de silencio, una persona indicada lee la letanía, página 276.

Letanía por la misión de la Iglesia

Luego el oficiante continúa con una de las siguientes, o alguna otra colecta apropiada.

Coleta para la fundación de una iglesia por iniciativa de una parroquia

Oh Dios, que inspiraste a los apóstoles en Jerusalén a que oraran y ayunaran para discernir tu voluntad: Envíanos tu Espíritu para que aprendamos lo que te gustaría que hiciéramos y las palabras y testimonio que deseas que ofrezcamos, para que tu reino venga y tu poder se manifieste en esta *(diócesis, ciudad, etc)*. Para la gloria de tu Nombre. *Amén.*

Para la fundación de una iglesia con modelo apostólico

Dios clemente, que enviaste a tu Hijo Jesús a proclamar las Buenas Nuevas del reino y por él inspiraste a otros a sembrar las semillas de tu Iglesia: Guíanos para continuar este trabajo; muéstranos el próximo lugar donde fundar una congregación; y danos los dones para cumplir tu voluntad. Te lo pedimos por Jesucristo nuestro Salvador. *Amén.*

Por la colaboración regional en la fundación de una iglesia

Oh Dios santísimo, que soplas tu Espíritu dador de vida, en las congregaciones de esta *(región)*, tú que nos llamas a reunirnos en espíritu misionero para difundir el evangelio: Muestra a tu pueblo con quién debemos ir y el camino que hemos de andar. Ayúdanos a entender los profundos deseos de sus corazones y capacítanos para alimentarlos mediante la viva presencia de Jesucristo nuestro Salvador, en cuyo poder enseñamos y en cuyo nombre oramos. *Amén.*

Por la fundación de una iglesia multicultural

Dios eterno, que has prometido la salvación a todos los pueblos y nos has ofrecido la visión de una gran multitud de gentes de todas las naciones y tribus y lenguas alrededor de tu trono, ayúdanos a traer esa visión a nuestro tiempo y lugar; disipa de nosotros todo prejuicio y arrogancia; capacítanos para que escuchemos y hablemos palabras nuevas de esperanza y alabanza. Por Jesucristo, la Palabra viva. *Amén.*

Para ser usada durante una celebración dominical por la congregación que está discerniendo

Señor Jesús, que nos encomendaste hacer discípulos y discípulas a todas las naciones y prometiste que siempre estarías con nosotros, guía a esta congregación para que pueda llegar a las personas que deseas y capacítanos para ser instrumentos de tu obra salvadora, para la gloria de Dios. *Amén.*

O *bien*

Dios bendito, que creas todas las cosas nuevas: Guíanos mientras descubrimos tu voluntad para fundar una nueva comunidad de la Palabra y del Sacramento, para que sea levadura para el pan del mundo y vino de alegría para los tristes corazones; una asamblea vigorosa para el servicio y alegre en la alabanza; y un pueblo que escucha y responde a tu presencia en medio de ellos. Por Jesucristo nuestro redentor y firme compañero. *Amén.*

Para escoger personas con la destreza necesaria para fundar una iglesia

Santo Espíritu, te deleitas en equiparnos con todos los dones del ministerio *(especialmente _____)* para que podamos extender el Reino de Dios: Levanta entre nosotros y sé con aquellos que llamas de entre nosotros para realizar esta nueva obra, de tal manera que el Cuerpo de Cristo crezca en poder y aptitud para la transformación del mundo; por Jesucristo nuestro Señor. *Amén.*

Padre Nuestro

Sigue la oración del Padrenuestro con esta u otra introducción

Uniendo nuestras oraciones en ésta, oremos como Jesús nos enseñó:

Padre nuestro...

El diácono, o el oficiante, despide al pueblo usando las siguientes u otras despedidas apropiadas:

Salgan en el nombre de Cristo.:
Vayan a la (ciudad, pueblo, region, barrios, vecindarios...)
de_____.
Vayan a sus propios barrios.
Vayan a otras tierras y lugares apartados.
Vayan donde el nombre de Dios es bien conocido y donde todavía no es conocido.
Vayan a quienes les dan la bienvenida y a quienes les rechazan.
Vayan al mundo y compartan la Buena Nueva del amor de Dios. [¡Aleluya, aleluya!]

Pueblo   Demos gracias a Dios. [¡Aleluya, aleluya!]

En Cuaresma se omiten las aleluyas. En la época pascual se incluyen.

Lo Concerniente al Rito

Esta liturgia se ha pensado para cuando un fundador de iglesia, un misionero o un grupo misionero, seleccionado y capacitado, va a ser enviado por la diócesis (y por la congregación patrocinadora), a un lugar reservado para una congregación. Si la nueva iglesia ya tiene nombre, hay oportunidades en la liturgia para ese caso. El rito se debe adaptar a las circunstancias de la misión.

Esta es una liturgia eucarística. Se da por entendido la participación del obispo o su representante, del clero y otros miembros de la(s) congregación(es) patrocinadora(s), del fundador de la iglesia y de su equipo, de los que han apoyado al equipo y de los miembros de la nueva iglesia.

Esta liturgia tiene sus raíces en los símbolos y teología del Bautismo, reconociendo que el trabajo de divulgar el evangelio y de edificar el Cuerpo de Cristo, que es la Iglesia, es una tarea de todos los bautizados. Con esto en mente, en esta liturgia se comisionan a determinados ministros y se reconocen sus responsabilidades.

Es apropiado adaptar estos ritos a constumbres locales de dialecto e idioma.

Liturgia para comisionar a un fundador de iglesia, a un misionero o a un grupo misionero

Se puede cantar una canción o un himno.

Se usa una aclamación inicial, tomada del Libro de Oración Común (página 219) o Enriching Our Worship I (página 50)

Luego, sigue de esta manera

Celebrante	Hay un Cuerpo y un Espíritu.
Pueblo	Hay una esperanza en el llamado de Dios.
Celebrante	Un Señor, una Fe, un Bautismo.
Pueblo	Un Dios y Padre de todos.

Se puede cantar una canción de alabanza.

Celebrante	El Señor sea con ustedes.
Pueblo	Y con tu espíritu.
Celebrante	Oremos.

Sigue una de las colectas siguientes, o la colecta del día, o una de las colectas para la Misión de la Iglesia (LOC páginas 175 y 706).

Para la fundación de una iglesia por iniciativa de una parroquia

Señor Jesucristo, que les diste a tus amigos las Buenas Nuevas de salvación y los enviaste a difundirlas a Jerusalén, a Judea y a todo el mundo. Acompáñanos ahora que enviamos a estos amigos y compañeros en tu servicio, para que tu reino pueda llegar con poder a _____ (*lugar o nombre de la nueva iglesia*). Para la gloria de tu Nombre. *Amén.*

Para la fundación de una iglesia con modelo apostólico

Dios clemente, que enviaste a tu Hijo Jesús a proclamar
a todo el mundo las Buenas Nuevas de tu reino y que por
él inspiraste a otros a sembrar las semillas de tu Iglesia.
Ayúdanos mientras continuamos tu obra. Da poder a tu
siervo(a) y a todos los que le apoyan y dale los dones para
cumplir tu voluntad. Te lo pedimos por Jesucristo nuestro
Salvador. *Amén.*

Por la colaboración regional en la fundación de una iglesia

Oh Dios santísimo, que soplas tu Espíritu de vida en las
congregaciones de esta (*región...*), y que nos llamas a
reunirnos en espíritu misionero para difundir el evangelio.
Bendícenos al comenzar este nuevo viaje, acompaña a
quienes hemos escogido para esta tarea y capacítalos para
que alimenten a tu pueblo en _____ mediante la viva
presencia de Jesucristo nuestro Salvador, en cuyo poder
enseñamos y en cuyo nombre oramos. *Amén.*

Por la fundación de una iglesia multicultural

Dios eterno, que has prometido la salvación a todos los
pueblos y nos has ofrecido la visión de una gran multitud
de gentes de todas las naciones y tribus y lenguas alrededor
de tu trono, ayúdanos mientras hacemos realidad esta
visión en nuestro tiempo y lugar; acompaña a quienes ahora
emprenden tu labor en _____; y capacítalos para que
escuchen y hablen palabras nuevas de esperanza y alabanza.
Por Jesucristo, la Palabra viva. *Amén.*

Por los fundadores de cualquier iglesia

Oh Dios santo, que escoges trabajadores para tu cosecha,
enviándolos como sembradores de tu Evangelio y cuidadores

de la nueva vida. Bendice a estos tus siervos en sus tareas de fundar y cuidar de tu Iglesia en _____; hazlos aptos para el servicio, anímalos con tu alegría, y ayúdalos a que se acuerden y confíen que eres tú quien da la cosecha. Por Jesucristo, el Salvador de las almas. *Amén.*

O bien

Bendito Dios, que creas luz de las tinieblas: Envía el poder de tu Espíritu sobre estos siervos(as) N. *(y N.)* que se disponen a llevar tu evangelio a _____. Que vayan llenos(as) de tu luz para que brillen con tu resplandor y atraigan a todo el mundo al brillo de tu amor y compasión. Por Jesús, nuestra luz y salvación. *Amén.*

Se lee uno o dos de los siguientes pasajes de las Sagradas Escrituras. Si se celebra la Comunión, las Lecturas concluyen siempre con un pasaje del Evangelio.

Josué 1:6-9 *(Vocación de Josué)*
Isaías 8:1-8 *(Vocación de Isaías)*
Jeremías 1:5-10 *(Vocación de Jeremías)*

Salmos: 65, 66; 100; 115; 147

Hechos 15:13-21 *(Separación de Pablo y Bernabé para el trabajo misionero)*
Hechos 16:6-10 *(Envío de Pablo a Macedonia)*
Hechos 18:1-4, 7-10 *(Cristo dice a Pablo en una visión: "Tengo un pueblo numeroso en esta ciudad)*
Romanos 15:13-21 *(El Dios de la esperanza os colme de todo gozo...)*
1 Corintios 3:5-12 *(Pablo planta, Apolo riega, y Dios da el crecimiento)*
2 Corintios 5:16-62 *(Somos embajadores de Cristo)*
Efesios 2:13-22 *(Predicó la paz a los que estaban lejos...)*

(Se puede cantar un himno o una canción)

Mateo 9:36-38 *(Jesús se compadece de la gente)*
Mateo 28:16-20 *(Id, haced discípulos a todas las gentes, bautizándolas...)*

Lucas 10:1-9 *(Rogad para que el Dueño de la mies envíe obreros)*
Lucas 24:44-50 *(El perdón de los pecados se predicará a todos los pueblos)*
Juan 4:34-38 *(Ved los campos, ya blanquean para la siega)*

El sermón

La comisión

El fundador -y grupo misionero- de la iglesia está delante del obispo o de su representante y representantes de la diócesis, de la(s) congregación(es) patrocinadora(s) y de otras personas según sea apropiado. Si ya existen miembros de la nueva congregación, deben estar con el grupo fundador.

El obispo o representante del obispo dice

Que el *vicario (misionero, grupo misionero…)* y miembros de la nueva congregación ____sean presentados ahora.

El rector de la parroquia misionera, o un representante de la diócesis, dice

Presento a N. para que sea comisionado como *fundador de una iglesia,* y para que sirva como *vicario* de _____ en la Diócesis de _____.

Obispo

¿Crees que está bien calificado y debidamente preparado para este ministerio?

El rector o representante diocesano   Sí lo creo.

Obispo   ¿N., en la presencia de esta congregación, te comprometes a este nuevo deber y responsabilidad?

Fundador Me comprometo.

Fundador   Presento a estas personas que representan a todos los que servirán conmigo en la fundación de esta nueva iglesia.

Obispo   Ustedes se están comprometiendo a este nuevo trabajo, ¿harán todo lo posible para apoyar la vida y misión de esta nueva congregación?

Los miembros del grupo misionero o la nueva congregación   Así lo haremos.

Entonces el obispo se dirige a toda la asamblea

Ustedes, testigos de este nuevo inicio, ¿apoyarán y orarán por N. *(estas personas)* y por la comunidad de _____ en este ministerio?

El pueblo   Así lo haremos.

Se pueden entregar símbolos apropiados al Nuevo ministerio.

Obispo   Unámonos a estas personas que aceptan este ministerio del evangelio y renovemos nuestro pacto bautismal.

El pacto bautismal

Obispo	Crees en Dios Padre?
Pueblo	Creo en Dios Padre todopoderoso,
	Creador del cielo y de la tierra.

Obispo	¿Crees en Jesucristo, el Hijo de Dios?
Pueblo	Creo en Jesucristo, su único Hijo, nuestro Señor.
	Fue concebido por obra y gracia del Espíritu Santo
	y nació de la Virgen María.
	Padeció bajo el poder de Poncio Pilato.
	Fue crucificado, muerto y sepultado.
	Descendió a los infiernos.
	Al tercer día resucitó de entre los muertos.
	Subió a los cielos
	y está sentado a la diestra de Dios Padre.
	Desde allí ha de venir a juzgar a vivos y muertos.

Obispo	¿Crees en Dios el Espíritu Santo?
Pueblo	Creo en el Espíritu Santo,
	la santa Iglesia católica,
	la comunión de los santos,
	el perdón de los pecados,
	la resurrección de los muertos,
	y la vida eterna.

Obispo	¿Continuarás en la enseñanza y comunión de los apóstoles, en la fracción del pan y en las oraciones?
Pueblo	Así lo haré con la ayuda de Dios.

Obispo	¿Perseverarás en resistir al mal, y cuando caigas en pecado, te arrepentirás y te volverás al Señor?
Pueblo	Así lo haré con la ayuda del Dios.

Obispo	¿Proclamarás por medio de la palabra y el ejemplo las Buenas Nuevas de Dios en Cristo?
Pueblo	Así lo haré con la ayuda de Dios.

Obispo	¿Buscarás y servirás a Cristo en todas las personas, amando a tu prójimo como a ti mismo?
Pueblo	Así lo haré con la ayuda de Dios.

Obispo	¿Lucharás por la justicia y la paz entre todos los pueblos, y respetarás la dignidad de todo ser humano?
Pueblo	Así lo haré, con la ayuda de Dios.

Obispo	Oremos a Dios por todo el mundo y por esta nueva congregación.

Una persona indicada dirige la letanía por la Misión de la Iglesia (página 276) o la siguiente letanía de acción de gracias.

Por la Iglesia universal, de la cual, oh Cristo, eres el fundamento y la piedra principal,
Gracias, Señor.

Por tu presencia cuando dos o tres se reúnen en tu nombre,
Gracias, Señor.

Por hacernos hijos tuyos por adopción y gracia, y nutrirnos cada día con el pan de vida,
Gracias, Señor.

Por el conocimiento de tu voluntad y la gracia para cumplirla,
Gracias, Señor.

Por el cumplimiento de nuestros deseos y peticiones como mejor nos convenga,
Gracias, Señor.

Por el perdón de nuestros pecados que nos restaura a la
compañía de los fieles,
Gracias, Señor.

Por la bendición de la vida y la gracia de tu bondad.
Gracias, Señor.

Por la fe y perseverancia de aquellos que han partido antes
que nosotros,
Gracias, Señor.

Por la compañía de (María la madre de Dios, los santos
apóstoles, el bendito N. y de) todos los santos,
Gracias, Señor.

*Después de un momento de oración en silencio, el obispo concluye de
esta manera*

Oh Dios, te alabamos por la redención del mundo mediante
la muerte y resurrección de Jesucristo. Te damos gracias
por derramar tu Espíritu sobre nosotros, constituyendo
unos apóstoles, a otros profetas, a otros evangelistas, a
otros pastores y maestros para capacitar a tu pueblo para
la edificación del Cuerpo de Cristo. Bendice esta obra que
emprendemos, para que tu Nombre sea glorificado, ahora y
por siempre. *Amén.*

La paz

La Eucaristía continúa con la Gran Plegaria Eucarística, el obispo o su representante, o rector de la parroquia misionera, presiden en el altar y los fundadores asisten de acuerdo a su orden.

Excepto en fiestas mayores, el prefacio es el de Pentecostés.

En lugar de la Oración usual de poscomunión, se puede decir la siguiente:

Celebrante u otra persona designada

Eterno Dios, dador de amor y vida, nos has nutrido con el Cuerpo y la Sangre de tu Hijo Jesucristo. Envíanos ahora al mundo para predicar las Buenas Nuevas, para hacer tu justicia y para caminar humildemente en tu senda.

Pueblo

Gloria sea a Dios, cuyo poder, actuando en nosotros, puede realizar tods las cosas infinitamente mejor de lo podemos pedir o pensar. Gloria a él en la Iglesia de generación en generación, y en Cristo Jesús por los siglos de los siglos. Amén.

El Obispo o el Celebrante pueden bendecir al pueblo.

Se puede usar la siguiente despedida u otra similar

Diácono o Celebrante	Salgamos al mundo para compartir las Buenas Nuevas del amor de Dios. [Aleluya, aleluya.]
Pueblo	Salimos en el Nombre de Cristo. [Aleluya, aleluya.]

En Cuaresma se omiten las aleluyas. En la época pascual se incluyen.

Lo *concerniente al Rito*

El rito de inauguración de una congregación es una celebración para los miembros de la nueva comunidad pero, todavía más importante, una oportunidad para mostrar hospitalidad a todos aquellos que buscan una iglesia a la cual asistir.

Es importante escoger un día apropiado dentro de la cultura que rodea a la nueva misión, por ejemplo, la fiesta de la Epifanía tiene significado especial en la comunidad hispana y es un día muy apto para captar la atención del pueblo. No se recomiendan días como el Domingo de Ramos, Pascua y Navidad. La experiencia demuestra que, en la mayoría de las circunstancias, las mejores fechas van de finales de agosto al último domingo de Pentecostés.

La congregación se reúne para servir a los que vienen por vez primera y debe ser consciente de la oportunidad de proclamar el Evangelio en la liturgia. Los miembros anfitriones se han de dar cuenta de la necesidad de la claridad y simplicidad. Es importante que una variedad de personas participe en el liderazgo del servicio.

Este rito da por entendido un contexto eucarístico. Se puede adaptar para un rito de la Palabra.

Si es apropiado, puede preceder inmediatamente a la Liturgia para reservar un espacio para el uso sagrado (página 275).

Es apropiado adaptar estos ritos a constumbres locales de dialecto e idioma.

Liturgia para la inauguración de una congregación

Reunión de la asamblea comunitaria

Se puede usar una de las siguientes, o una aclamación del Libro de Oración Común (página 245) o Enriching Our Worship I (página 50)

Oficiante/celebrante	Dios santo, que has llamado para ti a un pueblo:
Pueblo	Llénanos de tu presencia, afírmanos con tu amor.

O bien

Celebrante	Este es día que el Señor ha hecho;
Pueblo	Alegrémonos y gocémonos en él.

Oración de entrada   *La siguiente o se puede usar la colecta del día.*

Oficiante/celebrante	Oh Dios, fuente de todo principio: Te damos gracias por traernos a este nuevo día.
Pueblo	Envíanos tu Espíritu al comenzar este caminar como pueblo de_____[*nombre de la congregación*]. Capacítanos para proclamar las Buenas Nuevas de Jesús, protégenos de todo mal, y danos la gracia de vivir juntos en paz y oración común. Que en tu poder, lleguemos a ser una comunidad santa que transforme el mundo alrededor nuestro.

Oficiante/celebrante Te lo pedimos por Jesucristo, nuestro
Salvador, que vive y reina contigo y el
Espíritu Santo, un solo Dios, ahora
y por siempre. *Amén.*

La palabra

Lecturas: se pueden usar los propios del día o dos o más de las siguientes.

Antiguo Testamento

Éxodo 6:2-8 (Y os tomaré por pueblo mio)
Ezequiel 11:17-20 (Yo os recogeré de entre los pueblos)
Ezequiel 36:23b-30 (Entonces las naciones sabrán que yo soy el Señor.)

*Entre las Lecturas puede cantarse o decirse un Salmo, himno o cántico.
Son apropiados los Salmos 67 y 98.*

Epístola

2 Corintios 5: 16-21 (De modo que si alguno está en Cristo, nueva
criatura es.)
Hebreos 10. 19-25 (Mantengamos firme la profesión de nuestra
esperanza sin vacilar.)

Evangelio

Juan 13: 31-35 (que como yo os he amado, así también os améis los unos
a los oros.)
Mateo 11: 2-6 (Los ciegos reciben la vista y los cojos andan.)

A las lecturas sigue un sermón, homilía u otra reflexión.

Las oraciones

Se pueden ofrecer oraciones que pueden incluir

Una letanía por la Misión de la Iglesia *(página 276)*
Oraciones de los fieles *(LOC páginas 305-316)*
Intercesiones generales y acciones de gracias

La Eucaristía

Prefacio eucarístico: *el de Pentecostés; el de los apóstoles/ordenaciones;
u otro prefacio apropiado para la ocasión*

Oración después de la comunión: *son especialmente apropiadas las
que se encuentran en la páginas 261-262 de la liturgia para comisionar, en
Enriqueciendo nuestra Adoración I, página 69; o en el LOC, página 288*

Despedida

Oficiante/celebrante	Salgamos al mundo, gozándonos en el poder del Espíritu. [¡Aleluya, aleluya!]
Pueblo	Demos gracias a Dios [¡Aleluya, aleluya!]

En Cuaresma se omiten las aleluyas. En la época pascual se incluyen.

Lo Concerniente al Rito

Este rito se ha preparado para que lo use un equipo fundador o una congregación nueva que empieza a tener servicios en una localidad tal como una escuela, un asilo, o cualquier otro espacio secular. Adaptándolo se puede usar en otras varias situaciones, como cuando un grupo se reúne para un retiro en un hotel. Se espera que sea, pero no exclusivamente, un lugar o edificio regular con fines de adoración. Se podrían colocar en la habitación símbolos significativos cristianos, como una cruz, velas, un estandarte, etc. antes o durante el rito.

De entrada se puede cantar un himno, y, si es apropiado, la congregación y los ministros litúrgicos pueden ir en procesión hasta el lugar que va a ser dedicado.

Es apropiado adaptar estos ritos a constumbres locales de dialecto e idioma.

Reserva de un espacio secular para uso sagrado

Antífona

Tú, oh Señor, los traerás y los plantarás
en el santuario que has establecido.

V.   Todas tus obras te alaban, oh Dios,
R.   Y tus fieles siervos te bendicen.

O bien (especialmente si se acaba de colocar una cruz en el lugar)

V.   Mediante la cruz de Jesús,
R.   Nos hemos reunidos y reconciliado en Dios.

Oficiante   Oremos

Bendito seas, oh Dios, soberano del universo. Abundantes
son tus dones y con sabiduría has creado todas las cosas para
que te glorifiquen. Acompáñanos y bendícenos ahora que
dedicamos este espacio para tu gloria y honor. Precédenos
y acompáñanos siempre que te adoremos aquí. Revélate
en la Palabra que se nos hable y que escuchemos, en el
compañerismo mutuo y al partir el pan. Danos alegría en
todas tus obras, y concede que este espacio sea un lugar donde
siempre se cumpla tu palabra y tu nombre sea glorificado.
Lo pedimos por Jesucristo, nuestro Salvador, en el poder del
Espíritu *Amén.*

*En una celebración de la Eucaristía se puede cantar la Gloria in Excelsis
u otra canción de alabanza, mientras todos van ocupando su lugar para la
adoración. Seguirá la colecta del día o la colecta una liturgia de iniciación.
En un rito de Oración de la mañana o de la tarde o semejante, puede seguir
a la dedicación un salmo apropiado de invitatorio o un himno.*

Letanía por la misión de la Iglesia

Dios santo, en quien todas las cosas, en el cielo y en la tierra, tienen su ser,
Ten compasión de nosotros.

Jesús el Cristo, por quien el mundo se reconcilia con el Padre,
Ten compasión de nosotros.

Santo Espíritu, cuya gloria llena el mundo y escudriña las profundidades de Dios,
Ten compasión de nosotros.

Bendita Trinidad, fuente de unidad y diversidad,
Ten compasión de nosotros.

De corazones ciegos y espíritus mezquinos, que se niegan a ver la necesidad que la humanidad tiene de tu amor,
Líbranos, Salvador.

Del orgullo, la autosuficiencia y la falta de admisión sobre nuestra necesidad de tu compasión,
Líbranos Salvador.

Del desaliento ante el dolor y la decepción, y de la falta de persistencia y esmero,
Líbranos, Salvador.

De la ignorancia, de la apatía y complacencia, que nos impiden
difundir el evangelio,
Líbranos, Salvador.

Oh Dios, te rogamos por los dones del ministerio.
Inspira nuestras mentes con una visión de tu reinado para este
lugar y tiempo,
Escúchanos, oh Cristo.

Toca nuestros ojos para que veamos tu gloria en toda la
creación,
Escúchanos, oh Cristo.

Toca nuestros oídos para que oigamos de cada voz el hambre
de esperanza e historias estimulantes,
Escúchanos, oh Cristo.

Toca nuestros labios para que transmitamos en toda lengua y
dialecto las maravillosas obras de Dios,
Escúchanos, oh Cristo.

Toca nuestros corazones para que podamos discernir la misión
para la que nos llamas,
Escúchanos, oh Cristo.

Toca nuestros pies para que llevemos tus Buenas Nuevas a
nuestros barrios, comunidades y a todas las partes del mundo,
Escúchanos, oh Cristo.

Toca nuestras manos para que podamos cumplir la obra que
nos pides realizar,
Escúchanos, oh Cristo.

Fortalece y anima a todos los que ministran en tu nombre en lugares solitarios, peligrosos e ingratos,
Escúchanos, oh Cristo.

Abre los corazones y las manos de los que apoyan tu Iglesia en este y en todo lugar,
Escúchanos, oh Cristo.

La letanía concluye con una colecta, como las ofrecidas en las liturgias para fundar iglesias o una colecta por la mission de la Iglesia (LOC páginas 175, 706).

Varias colectas, bendiciones y oraciones, para fundaciones de iglesias

Estas colectas se pueden usar y adaptar a diferentes situaciones, como cuando se envía en misión a fundadores de iglesias, a evangelistas, a misioneros, a miembros de un comité de mayordomía, etc.

Oh Dios, creador y soberano de todas las cosas, tu reino crece como un grano de mostaza y se transforma en vida abundante: Bendice a quienes fundan y cuidan de la nueva vida de tu Iglesia, para que se convierta en un lugar acogedor, en un refugio de salvación, en una escuela para las almas, y en un manantial de vida. Te lo pedimos por Jesucristo, nuestra fortaleza y salvación. *Amén.*

Dios bendito, que haces todas las cosas nuevas: concede que esta joven comunidad de la Palabra y del Sacramento pueda ser levadura para el pan del mundo y vino de alegría para los tristes corazones; una asamblea vigorosa para el servicio y alegre en la alabanza; y un pueblo que escucha y responde a tu presencia en medio de ellos. Por Jesús, nuestro redentor y firme compañero. *Amén.*

Dios santo, que escoges trabajadores para tu cosecha, y los envías como sembradores de tus buenas nuevas, portadores de salud, y guardianes de nueva vida: Bendice a N. *(y a N.)* en su labor de fundar y cuidar de tu Iglesia *(en____)*; hazlos aptos para el servicio, anímalos con tu alegría, y ayúdalos a que se acuerden y confíen en que eres tú quien da la cosecha. Por Jesucristo, el Salvador de las almas. *Amén.*

Bendito Dios, que creas luz de las tinieblas: envía el poder de tu Espíritu sobre estos siervos *N. (y N.)* que se disponen a llevar tu Evangelio a_____. Que vayan llenos de tu luz para que brillen con tu resplandor, y atraigan a todo el mundo al deslumbre de tu amor y compasión. Por Jesús, nuestra luz y salvación. *Amén.*

Oh Jesús Salvador, que te nos diste a conocer al partir el pan y al darnos el vino para nuestra reconciliación: Danos ánimo en este trabajo misionero para que así como nosotros también somos partidos, derramados y repartidos, alimentando al mundo, encontremos en ti perfección. *Amén.*

Santísimo Dios, dador de toda vida: Los amigos de Jesús proclamaron las Buenas Nuevas cada uno en diferente lugar de acuerdo con sus dones y llamado. Bendice a *N. (y a N.)* que ahora proclaman tu palabra de amor, haciendo discípulos y discípulas para tu obra y edificando tu Iglesia; mediante el poder de tu Espírtu y en el Nombre de Cristo. *Amén.*

Oración de dedicación

Cristo Jesús, que nos acompañas en el caminar, eres nuestra luz y nuestro escudo; guía nuestro camino, sé nuestra clara visión, elévanos con la alegría de tu evangelio, y bendice el trabajo que hacemos en tu nombre y honor, porque tú eres nuestro amado, y nuestra nueva vida. *Amén.*

Himnos sugeridos para las liturgias relacionadas con la fundación de nuevas iglesias o misiones

Del *Hymnal 1982*

302/303 Father, we thank thee who hast planted
304 I come with joy to meet my Lord
521 Put forth, O God, thy Spirit's might
527 Singing songs of expectation
528 Lord, you give the great commission (Rowthorn)
530 Spread, O spread thou mighty Word
537 Christ for the world we sing!
576/577 God is love, and where true love is

De *Wonder, Love and Praise*

741 Filled with the Spirit's power
752 There's a sweet, sweet Spirit
761 All who hunger gather gladly
763 As we gather at your table
778 We all are one in mission
779 The church of Christ in every age
780 Lord, you give the great commission (Abbot's Leigh)
782 Gracious Spirit, give your servants
787 We are marching in the light of God
794 Muchos resplandores
796 Unidos
811 You shall cross the barren desert
812 I, the Lord of sea and sky
819 Guide my feet Lord

De *Lift Every Voice and Sing II*

50 The angel said to Philip
120 There's a sweet, sweet Spirit in this place
159 How to reach the masses
160 This little light of mine
161 "Go preach my gospel," saith the Lord

De *El Himnario*

2 Es tiempo de que alabemos a Dios
9 Todo se hace para la gloria de Dios
14 Grandes y maravillosas son tus obras
19 Señor, ¿qué es nuestro templo?
33 Cantemos al amor de los amores
56 Hay un dulce espíritu
205 Iglesia de Cristo, tu santa misión
209 Es Cristo de su Iglesia
213 ¡Suelta la alegría!
216 Muchos resplandores
223 Somos uno en espíritu
243 Una espiga
246 Te ofrecemos, Padre nuestro
252 Somos pueblo que camina
303 He decidido seguir a Cristo
306 Yo, el Dios de cielo y mar
312 A este santo templo
313 Tú has venido a la orilla (también enWLP 758)
317 Caminenos a la luz de Dios
321 Dios hoy nos llama

Concernant l'Office

Cet office a été créé pour aider les congrégations et les diocèses qui prennent en considération une nouvelle mission d'église, à percevoir la volonté du Saint-Esprit. L'office peut aussi être utilisé par une équipe qui se prépare pour la fondation d'une nouvelle église et/ou être incorporé à un ou plusieurs offices du dimanche par des congrégation(s) qui supportent ou parrainent la mission. L'office peut être utilisé pour initier une période de discernement intentionnel; et à d'autres points dans le cadre de ce processus.

L'office encourage le silence et le calme pour écouter le mouvement du Saint-Esprit. Ce n'est pas une liturgie eucharistique.

Il est approprié d'adapter ce rite à la coutume locale, à la langue, au dialecte et à l'idiome.

Discernement pour une nouvelle mission d'église

Officiant	Soyez tranquilles devant le Seigneur,
Peuple	Et attendez patiemment la présence de Dieu.

On garde une période de silence.

Officiant	Ô, Saint-Esprit, tu es la ressource et le guide de celui qui est en quête.
Peuple	Viens, crée, renouvelle et inspire.
Officiant	Enseigne-nous à entendre, enseigne-nous à parler.
Peuple	Montre-nous ta volonté pour que nous la suivions.

On lit une ou deux Leçons.
Une liste de leçons et psaumes suggérés

I Rois 3:3-10 (Dieu demande Salomon, « Demande ce que tu veux que je te donne » .)
Isaïe 49: 5-13 (Je t'établis pour être la lumière des nations, pour porter mon salut jusqu'aux...)
Ruth 1: 8-18. (Ton peuple sera mon peuple, et ton Dieu sera mon Dieu...)
Osée 6:1-6, 11-7:1a (À toi aussi, Juda, une moisson est préparée)

Psaumes: 37, 46

Matthieu 28:17-20 (Allez, faites de toutes les nations des disciples...)
Jean 5:25-39 (Je ne cherche pas ma volonté, mais la volonté de celui qui m'a envoyé.)
Éphésiens 1:1-14 (Car il nous a fait connaître... le mystère de sa volonté)

On garde une période significative de silence après chaque lecture des Saintes Écritures. Un sermon ou une homélie est découragée en faveur d'un moment de silence pour écouter le mouvement du Saint-Esprit.

Après la [seconde] période de silence, une personne désignée dirige les Litanies, page 308.

Litanies pour la mission de l'église

L'Officiant continue ensuite avec une des Collectes suivantes ou avec une autre qui soit appropriée.

Une collecte pour la fondation d'une église à l'initiative d'une paroisse

Ô Dieu, toi qui as inspiré tes apôtres à Jérusalem pour prier et jeûner afin de percevoir ta volonté: Envoie-nous ton Esprit, pour que nous apprenions ce que tu veux que nous fassions et les paroles et le témoignage que tu veux que nous t'offrions, pour que ton Royaume vienne et ta puissance soit révélée dans ce *(diocèse, doyenné, ville)*; à la gloire de ton Nom. *Amen.*

Une collecte pour la fondation d'une église selon le modèle apostolique

Père miséricordieux, toi qui as envoyé ton Fils Jésus à proclamer à tous la Bonne Nouvelle de ton Royaume et par lui as inspiré les individus à semer les graines de ton église: Guide-nous pour que nous continuions ce travail; montre-nous le champ suivant où planter; et donne-nous les dons pour accomplir ta volonté; nous te le demandons tout par Jésus, notre Sauveur. *Amen.*

Une collecte pour la collaboration régionale dans la fondation d'une église

Ô Dieu Saint, toi qui souffles ton Esprit donneur de vie dans les congrégations de cette *(région, doyenné, ...),* en nous appelant à nous réunir en mission pour répandre l'Évangile: Montre-nous les personnes auxquelles nous devons aller et le chemin sur lequel nous devons marcher; aide-nous à comprendre les profonds désirs de leurs cœurs et donne-nous le pouvoir de les nourrir par la présence vive de Jésus-Christ, notre Sauveur, dans la puissance duquel nous nous mettons et dans le nom duquel nous prions. *Amen.*

Une collecte pour la fondation d'une église multiculturelle

Dieu éternel, toi qui as promis le salut à tous les peuples et qui nous as donné une vision d'une grande multitude autour de ton trône, de toutes les nations et tribus et langues: Aide-nous à apporter cette vision à notre temps et lieu; bannis de nous tous les préjugés et les présomptions fausses; et donne-nous le pouvoir d'entendre et de parler de nouvelles paroles d'espérance et de louange; par Jésus-Christ, la Parole Vive. *Amen.*

Une collecte pour l'utilisation régulière pendant l'office de dimanche des congrégations en discernement

Seigneur Jésus, toi qui nous as commandé à faire des disciples de toutes les nations et qui as promis que tu seras toujours avec nous: Guide cette congrégation pour voir les peuples que tu veux que nous joignions et donne-nous le pouvoir d'être des instruments de ton travail sauveur, pour la gloire de Dieu. *Amen.*

ou

Dieu Béni, toi qui fais toute chose nouvelle: Guide-nous tandis que nous cherchons ta volonté pour une nouvelle communauté de la Parole et du Sacrement, pour qu'elle soit le levain du pain du monde et le vin de la joie pour les cœurs qui sont dans le besoin; une réunion forte pour le service et contente dans la louange; et un peuple qui écoute et qui répond à ta présence parmi eux; par Jésus, notre Rédempteur et compagnon dévoué. *Amen.*

Une collecte pour chercher des gens possédant les talents nécessaires pour la fondation d'une église

Saint-Esprit, toi qui prends plaisir à nous donner tous les dons pour l'office *(surtout___)* pour agrandir le Royaume de Dieu: Cherche parmi nous et donne du pouvoir à ceux que tu as choisis pour ce nouveau travail, pour que le Corps de Christ pousse en puissance et en santé, pour la transformation du monde; par Jésus-Christ, notre Seigneur. *Amen.*

Saint-Esprit, qui prends plaisir à nous donner tous les dons pour l'office *(surtout___)* pour agrandir le Royaume de Dieu: Cherche parmi nous et donne du pouvoir à ceux que tu as choisis pour ce nouveau travail, pour que le Corps de Christ pousse en puissance et en santé, pour la transformation du monde; par Jésus-Christ, notre Seigneur. *Amen.*

Notre Père

L'Officiant présente la prière avec cette proposition ou bien avec une autre.

Rassemblant toutes nos prières dans celle-ci, comme Jésus nous a enseigné, nous prions maintenant:

Notre Père...

Un diacre ou bien l'Officiant laisse sortir le peuple à l'aide de la formule suivante ou bien d'une autre qui soit appropriée

Sortez dans le nom de Christ.
Allez à la (*Ville, village, région...*) de _____.
Allez dans vos quartiers.
Allez à des campagnes et des lieux inconnus.
Allez là où le nom de Dieu est bien connu et là où il doit encore être connu.
Allez à ceux qui vous accueillent et à ceux qui vous rejettent.
Allez dans le monde et partagez la Bonne Nouvelle de l'amour de Dieu. [Alléluia, Alléluia !]

Le Peuple répond   Nous rendons grâce à Dieu. [Alléluia, Alléluia !]

En Carême, on omet les Alléluias. Dans la saison des Pâques, on les inclut.

Concernant l'Office

Cette liturgie est conçue pour être employée à l'occasion d'envoyer un fondateur d'église, un missionnaire et/ou une équipe de mission choisis et instruits par un diocèse (et une congrégation de support), à un endroit/ congrégation désigné. Si la nouvelle église a déjà un nom, il y a des possibilités dans la liturgie pour cette désignation-là. L'office doit être adapté aux circonstances de la mission.

C'est une liturgie eucharistique. Elle présuppose la participation de l'évêque diocésain ou du représentant de l'évêque; du clergé et d'autres membres des congrégation(s) de support; et du fondateur de l'église et son équipe, leurs partisans et les membres de la nouvelle église.

La liturgie a ses racines dans les images et la théologie du Baptême, reconnaissant que le travail de répandre l'Évangile et de construire l'Église du Corps de Christ est le travail de toutes les personnes baptisées. Avoir compris cela, des ministres particuliers sont mis en service et leurs responsabilités sont reconnues dans cette liturgie.

Il est approprié d'adapter ce rite à la coutume locale, à la langue, au dialecte et à l'idiome.

Une liturgie pour mettre en service un fondateur d'église, un missionnaire ou une équipe missionnaire

On peut chanter un hymne ou un motet

On emploie une Acclamation Initiale Le Livre de la Prière Commune(page 207) ou Enriching our Worship I (Enrichir notre adoration) (page 50)

Ensuite il y a

Célébrant Il n'y a qu'un Corps et qu'un Esprit;
Peuple Il n'y a qu'une espérance dans l'appel que Dieu nous fait;
Célébrant Un seul Seigneur, une seule Foi, un seul Baptême;
Peuple Un seul Dieu et Père de tous.

On peut chanter une chanson de louange.

Célébrant Le Seigneur soit avec vous.
Peuple Et avec ton esprit.
Célébrant Prions le Seigneur.

Il suit une des collectes suivantes; ou la Collecte du Jour; ou bien une des collectes pour la Mission de l'Église (LPC pages 166, 666).

Pour la fondation d'une église à l'initiative de la paroisse

Seigneur Christ, toi qui as préparé tes amis et les as envoyés à porter la Bonne Nouvelle du salut, de Jérusalem à Judée et partout dans le monde: Sois présent lorsque nous envoyons ces amis et compagnons à ton service, pour que ton Royaume vienne avec puissance à ____ [*endroit ou nom de la nouvelle église*]; à la gloire de ton Nom. *Amen.*

Pour la fondation d'une église selon le modèle apostolique

Dieu Miséricordieux, toi qui as envoyé ton Fils Jésus à proclamer à tous la Bonne Nouvelle de ton Royaume et par lui as inspiré les individus à semer les graines de ton église: Aide-nous lorsque nous continuons ce travail. Donne pouvoir à *N.*, ton serviteur et à tous ceux qui l'appuient et donne leur les dons pour accomplir ta volonté; nous te le demandons tout par Jésus, notre Sauveur. *Amen.*

Pour la collaboration régionale dans la fondation d'une église

Ô Dieu Saint, toi qui souffle ton Esprit donneur de vie dans les congrégations de cette (*région, doyenné, ...*), en nous appelant à nous réunir dans la mission pour répandre l'Évangile: Bénis-nous lorsque nous commençons ce nouveau voyage; va avec ceux que tu as choisis pour ce travail; et donne leur le pouvoir de nourrir ton peuple à ____ par la présence vive de Jésus-Christ, notre Sauveur, dans le pouvoir duquel nous nous mettons et au Nom duquel nous prions. *Amen.*

Une collecte pour la fondation d'une église multiculturelle

Dieu Éternel, toi qui as promis le salut à tous les peuples et qui nous as donné une vision d'une grande multitude autour de ton trône, de toutes les nations et les tribus et les langues: Aide-nous lorsque nous apportons cette vision dans notre temps et lieu; accompagne ceux qui maintenant entreprennent ton travail à ____; et donne leur le pouvoir d'entendre et de parler de nouvelles paroles d'espérance et de louange; par Jésus-Christ, la Parole vivante. *Amen.*

Pour les fondateurs de toute église

Ô Dieu Saint, toi qui choisis des ouvriers pour ta moisson, en les envoyant en tant que semeurs de ton Évangile et des gardiens de la nouvelle vie: Bénis *ces serviteurs à toi* dans *leur* travail de fonder et de soigner ton Église à ____; prépare-*les* pour le service, anime-*les* avec ta joie et aide-*les* à se souvenir et à croire que c'est toi qui apporteras la moisson; par Jésus-Christ, le Sauveur des âmes. *Amen.*

ou

Dieu Béni, toi qui suscite la lumière du noir: Envoie le pouvoir de ton Esprit sur tes serviteurs N. *(et N.)* lorsqu'*ils* portent ton Évangile à _____. Qu'*ils* soient pleins de ta lumière et qu'*ils* brillent avec ton éclat, en attirant à tous vers l'éclat de ton amour et merci; par Jésus, notre Sauveur et la vraie Lumière. *Amen.*

Ensuite on lit un ou plusieurs des passages suivants des Saintes Écritures. D'autres passages particulièrement appropriés pour le jour peuvent être remplacés. S'il y a une Communion, un passage de l'Évangile conclut toujours les lectures.

Josué 1:6-9 *(vocation de Josué)*
Isaïe 6: 1-8 *(vocation d'Isaïe)*
Jérémie: 1:5-10 *(vocation de Jérémie)*

Psaumes: 65, 66; 100; 115; 147

Actes: 13:1-4 *(séparation de Paul et Barnabas pour la fondation d'une église)*
Actes: 16:6-10 *(Appel de Paul à Macédoine)*
Actes: 18:1-4, 7-10 *(La vision de Christ de Paul à Corinthe: « j'ai un peuple nombreux dans cette ville »)*
Romains 15:13-21 *(Que le Dieu de l'espérance vous remplisse de toute joie ...)*
I Corinthiens 3:5-12 *(Paul plante, Apollos arrose et Dieu fait croître)*
II Corinthiens 5:16-6:2 *(Nous sommes les ambassadeurs de Christ.)*
Ephésiens 2:13-22 *(Il a annoncé la paix à ceux qui étaient loin...)*

On peut chanter un hymne, un psaume ou un motet.

Matthieu 9: 36-38 *(Jésus est ému de compassion pour les gens)*
Matthieu 28:16-20 *(Allez, faites de toutes les nations des disciples, les baptisant...)*
Luc 10:1-9 *(Priez donc le maître de la moisson d'envoyer des ouvriers.)*
Luc 24:44-50 *(Le pardon des péchés sera prêché à tous les peuples)*
Jean 4:34-38 *(Regardez les champs qui déjà blanchissent pour la moisson)*

Le Sermon

La mise en service

Le fondateur/l'équipe de l'église est devant l'évêque ou le représentant de l'évêque et les représentants du diocèse, des congrégations de support et d'autres personnes comme approprié. S'il y a des membres de la nouvelle congrégation déjà identifiés, ils doivent être avec l'équipe de fondateurs.

L'évêque ou le représentant de l'évêque dit

Le *pasteur (missionnaire, équipe...)* et les membres de la nouvelle congrégation _____ seront présentés maintenant.

Le curé de la paroisse missionnaire ou un représentant diocésain dit

Je présente N. pour être mis en service en tant que *fondateur de l'église* et pour qu'il serve en tant que *pasteur* de _____ du Diocèse de _____.

L'évêque dit

Croyez-vous qu'*elle* soit bien qualifiée et dûment préparée pour ce ministère ?

Le curé ou le représentant diocésain répond   Oui, je le crois bien.

Évêque   N., est-ce que tu, dans la présence de cette congrégation, t'engages à cette nouvelle confiance et responsabilité ?

Fondateur   Oui.

Fondateur   Je présente ces personnes qui représenteront tous ceux qui serviront avec moi dans la fondation de cette nouvelle église.

Évêque   Est-ce que vous, ceux qui vous engagez à ce nouveau travail ferez tout le possible pour appuyer la vie et la mission de cette nouvelle congrégation ?

Les membres de l'équipe et/ou de la nouvelle congrégation Oui, nous le ferons.

L'évêque se dirige ensuite à toute l'assemblée

Est-ce que vous, qui êtes les témoins de ce commencement, appuierez et soutiendrez *N. (ces personnes)* et la communauté de ____ dans ce ministère ?

Peuple   Oui, nous le ferons.

Les symboles appropriés du nouveau ministère peuvent être offerts.

Évêque   Joignons ceux qui acceptent ce ministère de l'Évangile et renouvelons notre propre alliance baptismale.

L'Alliance baptismale

Évêque   Croyez-vous en Dieu, le Père ?
Peuple   Je crois en Dieu, le Père tout-puissant,
            créateur du ciel et de la terre.
Évêque   Croyez-vous en Jésus-Christ, le Fils de Dieu ?
Peuple   Je crois en Jésus-Christ, son Fils unique, notre Seigneur.
            Il a été conçu du Saint-Esprit
                et né de la Vierge Marie.
            Il a souffert sous Ponce Pilate,
                a été crucifié, est mort est a été enseveli.
            Il est descendu aux enfers.
            Le troisième jour est ressuscité d'entre les morts.
            Il est monté aux cieux,
                est assis à la droite de Dieu le Père tout-puissant.
            Il viendra juger les vivants et les morts.

Évêque   Croyez-vous au Saint-Esprit ?
Peuple   Je crois au Saint-Esprit,
                la sainte Église catholique,
                la communion des saints,
                la rémission des péchés,
                la résurrection de la chair,
                et la vie éternelle.

Évêque   Serez-vous assidus à l'enseignement des apôtres, à la
            communion fraternelle, à la fraction du pain et aux
            prières ?
Peuple   Oui, avec l'aide de Dieu.

Évêque   Persévérerez-vous à résister au mal et quand tu
            tomberas dans le péché vous repentirez-vous et
            retournerez-vous au Seigneur ?
Peuple   Oui, avec l'aide de Dieu.

Évêque	Proclameres-vous, tant par vos paroles que par votre exemple, la Bonne Nouvelle de Dieu manifestée en Jésus-Christ ?
Peuple	Oui, avec l'aide de Dieu.
Évêque	Chercherez-vous, pour le servir, le Christ dans les personnes que vous rencontrerez, et aimerez-vous votre prochain comme vous-mêmes ?
Peuple	Oui, avec l'aide de Dieu.
Évêque	Etes-vous prêts à lutter pour la justice et la paix parmi tous les peuples et à respecter la dignité de chaque être humain ?
Peuple	Oui, avec l'aide de Dieu.

Évêque Prions Dieu pour tout le monde et pour cette nouvelle congrégation.

Une personne assignée dirige les Litanies pour la Mission de l'Église (page 308) ou les Litanies suivantes pour l'action de grâces.

Pour l'Église universelle, de laquelle tu, Ô Christ, es la fondation et la pierre angulaire principale,
Nous te remercions, Seigneur.

Pour ta présence où que deux ou trois personnes se réunissent dans ton Nom,
Nous te remercions, Seigneur.

Pour nous faire tes enfants par adoption et grâce, et nous revigorer chaque jour avec le pain de la vie.
Nous te remercions, Seigneur.

Pour la connaissance de ta volonté et la grâce de l'accomplir,
Nous te remercions, Seigneur.

Pour l'accomplissement de nos désirs et pétitions comme il soit mieux pour nous,
Nous te remercions, Seigneur.

Pour le pardon de nos péchés, qui nous remet dans la compagnie de ton peuple fidèle,
Nous te remercions, Seigneur.

Pour la bénédiction de la vie avec ta bonté,
Nous te remercions, Seigneur.

Pour la foi et la persévérance de ceux qui sont partis avant nous,
Nous te remercions, Seigneur.

Pour la compagnie de (Marie la Porteuse de Dieu, les saints apôtres, le béni *N.* et de) tous les saints,
Nous te remercions, Seigneur.

Après une période de prière en silence, l'Évêque conclut avec les suivants:

Ô Dieu, nous te louons pour la rédemption du monde par la mort et la résurrection de Jésus le Christ. Nous te remercions pour verser ton Esprit sur nous, faisant des apôtres, des prophètes, des évangélisateurs, des pasteurs et des enseignants pour préparer ton peuple pour la construction du Corps de Christ. Bénis ce nouveau travail que nous entreprenons, pour que ton Nom soit glorifié, maintenant et pour toujours. *Amen.*

La Paix

*L'Eucharistie continue avec la Grande Prière d'Action de Grâces,
l'Évêque ou le représentant de l'Évêque, ou le Curé de la paroisse
missionnaire, présidant à la table et les fondateurs assistant
conformément à leur ordre.*

À l'exception des grandes fêtes, la Préface est celle de Pentecôte.

*Au lieu de la prière habituelle qui suit la communion, on peut dire la
suivante*

Célébrant ou une autre personne assignée

Éternel Donneur d'amour et de vie, tu nous as nourris avec
le Corps et le Sang de ton Fils Jésus-Christ. Envoie-nous
maintenant dans le monde pour prêcher ta Bonne Nouvelle,
pour faire ta justice et pour marcher humblement sur ton
chemin.

Peuple

Gloire à Dieu dont le pouvoir qui agit en nous peut faire
infiniment plus que nous ne pouvons demander ou nous
imaginer. Gloire à Dieu de génération en génération, dans
l'Église et en Jésus-Christ pour les siècles des siècles. Amen.

L'Évêque ou le Célébrant peut bénir le peuple.

On emploie cette formule de Sortie ou bien une autre

Diacre ou Célébrant Allez au monde et partagez la Bonne
                       Nouvelle de l'amour de Dieu.
                       [Alléluia, alléluia.]
Peuple   Nous y allons au Nom du Christ.
                       [Alléluia, alléluia.]

On omet les alléluias en Carême. On les emploie dans la Saison des Pâques.

Concernant l'Office

L'office d'inauguration d'une nouvelle congrégation est une célébration pour les membres de la nouvelle communauté, mais plus important encore, une occasion pour eux de montrer de l'hospitalité à ceux cherchant une église dans la communauté plus large.

Il est important de choisir un jour approprié pour la culture entourant la nouvelle mission Đ par exemple, la fête de l'Épiphanie a une importance particulière dans la communauté hispanique, et une date efficace pour un lancement public. Le Dimanche des Rameaux, de Pâques et le jour de Noël sont déconseillés. L'expérience montre que les dates entre la fin août et le Dernier Dimanche après la Pentecôte sont appropriées dans la plupart des contextes.

La congrégation se réunit pour servir ceux qui viennent pour la première fois et devraient être conscients des occasions de proclamer l'Évangile dans la liturgie. Les membres hôtes devraient être consciencieux du besoin de simplicité et de clarté. Il est important qu'une variété de personnes participe à la conduite de l'office.

Cet office assume un contexte eucharistique. Il peut être adapté à un office de la Parole.

S'il est approprié, la Liturgie pour Réserver un Espace Séculaire pour l'Usage Sacré (page 307) peut précéder l'office immédiatement.

Il est approprié d'adapter ce rite à la coutume locale, à la langue, au dialecte et à l'idiome.

Une liturgie pour l'inauguration d'une nouvelle congrégation

La Réunion

On peut employer une des suivantes ou une Acclamation d'Inauguration Le Livre de la Prière Commune(page 207) ou bien Enriching Our Worship I (Enrichir notre adoration) (page 50)

Officiant/Célébrant	Saint Dieu, tu as appelé pour toi-même un peuple.
Peuple	Remplis-nous de ta présence, affirme-nous avec ton amour.

ou

Officiant/Célébrant	C'est le jour que le Seigneur a fait.
Peuple	Réjouissons-nous et soyons contents en lui.

Prière d'Ouverture

On peut employer la collecte suivante ou bien la Collecte du Jour.

Officiant/Célébrant	Ô Dieu, la source de tous les commencements: nous te remercions pour nous apporter à ce nouveau jour.
Peuple	Envoie-nous ton Esprit lorsque nous commençons notre voyage comme le peuple de _____ *[nom de la congrégation].*

Prépare-nous pour proclamer la Bonne
Nouvelle de Jésus,
protège-nous de tous les maux,
et donne-nous la grâce de vivre ensemble
en paix et prière commune.
Pour que, dans ta puissance, nous
devenions une communauté sainte
qui transforme le monde autour de nous.

Officiant/Célébrant   Nous te le prions tout par Jésus-Christ,
notre Sauveur, qui vit et règne avec toi et le
Saint-Esprit, un Dieu, pour les siècles des
siècles. *Amen.*

La Parole

*On peut employer les Propres du Jour ou bien deux ou plusieurs des
suivants.*

De l'Ancien Testament
Exode 6:2-8 (Je vous prendrai pour mon peuple)
Ezéchiel 11:17-20 (Je vous recueillerai des pays)
Ezéchiel 36:23b-30 (les nations sauront que je suis le Seigneur)

*Entre les lectures, on peut chanter ou dire un psaume, un hymne ou un
cantique. Les Psaumes appropriés sont 67 et 98.*

Du Nouveau Testament
2 Corinthiens 5:16-21 (Si quelqu'un est en Christ, il est une nouvelle
créature)
Hébreux 10:19-25 (Retenons fermement la profession de notre
espérance)

L'Évangile

Jean 13:31-35 (comme je vous ai aimés, vous aussi, aimez-vous les uns les autres)
Matthieu 11:2-6 (les aveugles voient, les boiteux marchent)

Après les lectures, il suit un sermon, une homélie ou une autre réflexion.

Prières du peuple

Ici on offre des prières qui peuvent inclure

Une Litanie pour la Mission de l'Église *(page 308)*
Des Prières du Peuple *(telles que LPC pages 284-294)*
Des intercessions et des actions de grâces générales

À l'Eucharistie

Préface *On emploie la Préface pour la Pentecôte, pour les Apôtres et les Ordinations ou une autre préface appropriée pour l'occasion.*

Prières après la communion *Les prières spécialement appropriées sont les prières trouvées à la page 286-287 de la liturgie de mise en service; dans Enrichir notre adoration I, page 69; dans le LPC, page 267.*

Sortie

Officiant/Célébrant   Allons dans le monde, joyeux de la puissance de l'Esprit. [Alléluia, alléluia.]

Peuple   Nous rendons grâce à Dieu. [Alléluia, alléluia.]

En Carême on omet les alléluias. Dans la Saison des Pâques, on les inclut.

Concernant l'Office

Ce rite est conçu pour être utilisé par une équipe fondatrice d'une église ou par une nouvelle congrégation, qui commence le culte dans un lieu tel qu'une école, une maison de retraite, une « vitrine » ou tout autre espace séculaire. Avec de l'adaptation il pourrait être employé dans une variété d'autres situations, telles que le rassemblement initial d'un groupe de retraite dans un hôtel. Il prévoit l'utilisation régulière mais non exclusive de la salle ou du bâtiment pour le culte. Il peut être souhaitable de placer dans la salle des symboles significatifs de culte chrétien, tels qu'une croix, des bougies, une banderole etc. avant ou pendant le service.

Un hymne d'entrée peut être chanté et la congrégation et les ministres liturgiques peuvent aller en procession à l'emplacement de dédicace, si approprié. Une grande croix peut être placée dans un endroit visible à tous.

Il est approprié d'adapter ce rite à la coutume locale, à la langue, au dialecte et à l'idiome.

Réserver un espace séculaire pour l'usage sacré

Antienne

Tu les apporteras et les planteras, Ô Seigneur,
dans le sanctuaire que tu as établi.

V.   Tout ton travail te loue, Ô Dieu,
R.   Et tes serviteurs fidèles te bénissent.

ou (surtout si on vient d'installer une croix)

V.   Par la Croix de Jésus,
R.   Nous avons été rapprochés et réconciliés en Dieu.

Officiant   Prions le Seigneur.

Béni sois tu, Ô Dieu, roi de l'univers. Tes dons sont nombreux et
avec sagesse tu as créé toutes les choses pour qu'elles te donnent
de la gloire. Sois avec nous et bénis-nous tandis que nous
dédions cet *espace* à ta louange et honneur. Aussi souvent que
nous t'adorons ici, précède-nous et reste avec nous. Sois connu
pour nous dans la Parole dite et entendue, dans la fraternité
d'entre nous et dans la fraction du pain. Donne-nous de la joie
dans tous tes travaux et reconnais que cet *espace* soit un lieu où
ta volonté est faite et ton nom est glorifié; par Jésus-Christ, notre
Sauveur, dans le pouvoir du Saint-Esprit, nous prions. *Amen.*

Dans la célébration de l'Eucharistie, on peut chanter Gloria in Excelsis *ou
une autre Chanson de Louange, tandis que tous prennent leurs places pour
l'adoration. Il suivrait la Collecte du Jour ou la Collecte pour une Liturgie
d'Inauguration. Dans un office du soir/du matin ou un autre similaire, un
psaume Invitatoire approprié ou un hymne peuvent suivre la dédicace.*

Une litanie pour la mission de l'Église

Saint Dieu, dans lequel toutes les choses des cieux et de la terre ont leur être,
Prends pitié de nous.

Jésus le Christ, par qui le monde est réconcilié avec le Père,
Prends pitié de nous.

Saint-Esprit, dont la gloire remplit le monde et recherche les profondeurs de Dieu,
Prends pitié de nous.

Trinité Bénie, source d'unité et de diversité,
Prends pitié de nous.

Des cœurs aveugles et des esprits mesquins, qui refusent de voir la nécessité de toute l'humanité pour ton amour,
Sauveur, délivre-nous.

De la fierté, de l'autosuffisance et de la réticence à admettre notre propre besoin de ta compassion,
Sauveur, délivre-nous.

Du découragement devant la douleur et la déception et du manque de persévérance et de minutie,
Sauveur, délivre-nous.

De l'ignorance, de l'apathie et de la suffisance qui nous empêchent de répandre l'Évangile,
Sauveur, délivre-nous.

Ô Dieu, nous prions pour les dons du ministère.
Inspire nos esprits avec une vision de ton royaume dans ce temps et ce lieu.
Entends-nous, Ô Christ.

Touche nos yeux, pour que nous voyions ta gloire dans toute la création.
Entends-nous, Ô Christ.

Touche nos oreilles, pour que nous entendions de chaque bouche la faim d'espérance et des histoires de repos.
Entends-nous, Ô Christ.

Touche nos lèvres, pour que nous parlions dans toutes les langues et tous les dialectes des travaux merveilleux de Dieu.
Entends-nous, Ô Christ.

Touche nos coeurs, pour que nous percevions la mission à laquelle tu nous appelles.
Entends-nous, Ô Christ.

Touche nos pieds, pour que nous portions ta Bonne Nouvelle dans nos quartiers, communautés et dans tous les parts du monde.
Entends-nous, Ô Christ.

Touche nos mains, pour que nous puissions chacun accomplir le travail que tu nous donnes à faire.
Entends-nous, Ô Christ.

Renforce et encourage tous ceux qui desservissent dans ton nom, dans des endroits solitaires, dangereux et peu réceptifs.
Entends-nous, Ô Christ.

Ouvre les cœurs et les mains de beaucoup de gens pour appuyer ton Église dans ce et dans tout endroit.
Entends-nous, Ô Christ.

La Litanie conclut avec une collecte, telle que celles qui sont offertes dans les Liturgies pour Fonder une Église ou une collecte pour la Mission de l'Église (LPC pages 166, 666).

Une variété de collectes, de bénédictions et d'autres prières pour la fondation d'une église

Ces collectes peuvent être employées et adaptées pour une variété de situations, telles que lorsqu'on choisit des fondateurs d'églises, des évangélisateurs, des missionnaires, des membres d'un comité de direction, etc.

Ô Dieu, le Créateur et le roi de toutes les choses, ton règne pousse comme une graine de moutarde et devient une vie abondante: Bénis ceux qui plantent et soignent la nouvelle vie de ton Église, pour qu'elle puisse devenir un lieu de bienvenue, un refuge de guérison, une école pour les âmes et une source vitale; nous te le demandons tout par Jésus-Christ, notre pouvoir et notre salut. *Amen.*

Dieu Béni, qui crée toute chose nouvelle: reconnais que cette communauté jeune de la Parole et du Sacrement soit du levain pour le pain du monde et du vin pour la joie des cœurs qui sont dans le besoin; une réunion forte pour le service et contente dans la louange; et un peuple qui écoute et répond à ta présence parmi eux; par Jésus, notre rédempteur et compagnon dévoué. *Amen.*

Tu choisis des ouvriers pour ta moisson, Saint Dieu, et tu les envoies comme semeurs de ta bonne nouvelle, des ouvriers de guérison et des gardiens de la nouvelle vie: Bénis N. *(et N.)* dans *leur* travail de fonder et de soigner ton Église *(de ____);* prépare-*les* pour l'office, anime-*les* de ta joie et aide-*les* à se rappeler et à avoir confiance que c'est toi qui apporteras la moisson; par Jésus-Christ, le Sauveur des âmes. *Amen.*

Dieu Béni, toi qui suscites la lumière du noir: envoie le pouvoir de ton Esprit sur tes serviteurs *N. (et N.)* lorsqu'*ils* portent ton Évangile à _____. Qu'*ils* soient pleins de ta lumière et qu'*ils* brillent avec ton éclat, en attirant à tous vers l'éclat de ton amour et merci; par Jésus, notre Sauveur et la vraie Lumière. *Amen.*

Jésus, notre Sauveur, que nous t'avons connu dans la fraction du pain et dans le vin versé pour notre réconciliation: Donne-nous de bon courage pour ce travail de mission pour que nous soyons aussi rompus, versés et partagés pour l'alimentation du monde, nous nous rencontrons complets en toi. *Amen.*

Dieu Très Saint et Donneur de vie: Les amis de Jésus ont porté ta bonne nouvelle, chacun à un endroit différent selon leurs dons et vocation. Bénis *N. (et N.)* tandis qu'ils portent ta parole d'amour, faisant des disciples pour ton office et construisant ton Église; par le pouvoir de ton Esprit et dans le Nom de Jésus. *Amen.*

Une prière de dédicace

Christ Jésus, toi qui marches devant et derrière *nous/moi*, tu es *notre* lumière et *notre* bouclier; guide *notre* chemin, sois *notre* vision claire, lève-nous dans la joie de ton Évangile et bénis le travail que *nous* faisons dans ton nom et honneur, parce que tu es notre bien-aimé et *notre* vie nouvelle. *Amen.*

Hymnes suggérés pour les liturgies de fondation de nouvelles églises

De *Hymnal 1982* (du Recueil de cantiques, 1982)

302/303 Père nous te remercions à toi qui as planté
304 Je viens avec joie te rencontrer, mon Seigneur
521 Envoie, Ô Dieu, le pouvoir de ton Esprit
527 Chantant des chansons d'attente
528 Seigneur, tu donnes le grand service (Rowthorn)
530 Répands, Ô répands ta Parole puissante
537 Christ pour le monde nous chantons !
576/577 Dieu est l'amour et qui se trouve là où est le vrai amour

De *Wonder, Love and Praise* (Merveille, Amour et Louange)

741 Rempli du pouvoir de l'Esprit
752 Il y a un Esprit doux, doux
761 Tous ceux qui ont faim se réunissent volontiers
763 Quand nous nous réunissons à ta table
778 Nous sommes tous un dans la mission
779 L'église de Christ dans chaque âge
780 Seigneur, tu nous donnes la grande mission (Abbot's Leigh)
782 Esprit Miséricordieux, donne tes serviteurs
787 Nous marchons dans la lumière de Dieu
794 Beaucoup d'éclats
796 Unis
811 Tu traverseras le désert aride
812 Moi, le Seigneur de la mer et des cieux
819 Guide mes pieds, Seigneur

De *Lift Every Voice and Sing II* (Levez chaque voix et chantez II)

Restoring of Things Profaned

When a church building, altar, font, or other objects that have been set apart or consecrated, have been profaned, they may be restored to sacred use with the following form.

The bishop, or a priest, with such attendants as are appropriate, may go in procession around the exterior or interior of the church, or chapel, and then go to each object that has been profaned.

During the procession, Psalm 118 may be sung or said, with the following antiphon

I saw water proceeding out of the temple; from the right side it flowed, alleluia; and all those to whom that water came shall be saved, and shall say, alleluia, alleluia.

After the procession, each profaned object is addressed, and may be symbolically cleansed by the use of signs of purification, such as water or incense. The Celebrant touches or extends a hand toward each object and says

I declare this _____ restored to the use for which it has been dedicated and consecrated.

Then the Celebrant, standing in the midst of the church, says

Our help is in the Name of the Lord:
People   The maker of heaven and earth.

Celebrant	The Lord be with you.
People	And also with you.

Celebrant   Let us pray.   *(Silence)*

Almighty God, by the radiance of your Son's appearing you
have purified a world corrupted by sin: We humbly pray that
you would continue to be our strong defense against the
attacks of our enemies; and grant that [*this* _____
and] whatsoever in this *church* has been stained or defiled
through the craft of Satan or by human malice, may be
purified and cleansed by your abiding grace; that this place,
purged from all pollution, may be restored and sanctified, to
the glory of your Name; through Jesus Christ our Lord, who
lives and reigns with you and the Holy Spirit, one God, now
and for ever. *Amen.*

Secularizing a Consecrated Building

The Altar(s) and all consecrated and dedicated objects that are to be preserved are removed from the building before the service begins.

The bishop, or a minister appointed by the bishop, presides.

The clergy of the congregation, the churchwardens, and other persons who desire to participate, assemble in the building.

The Presiding Minister, using these or similar words, says

We who are gathered here know that this building, which has been consecrated and set apart for the ministry of God's holy Word and Sacraments, will no longer be used in this way, but will be taken down (used for other purposes).

To many of you this building has been hallowed by cherished memories, and we know that some will suffer a sense of loss. We pray that they will be comforted by the knowledge that the presence of God is not tied to any place or building.

The *Altar has* been removed and protected from desecration.

It is the intention of the diocese that the congregation which worshiped here will not be deprived of the ministry of Word and Sacrament.

Let the [bishop's] Declaration of Secularization now be read.

Then a Warden, or other person appointed, reads the bishop's Declaration, which is to be in the following form

In the Name of the Father, and of the Son, and of the Holy Spirit. *Amen.*

On the _____ day of _____, in the year of our Lord _____, by *N.N.*, Bishop of _____, this building was duly dedicated and consecrated in honor of _____ [and named _____].

The Sentence of Consecration has been in effect until this present date.

I, *N.N.*, Bishop of _____, do hereby revoke the said Sentence [issued by my predecessor], and do remit this building, and all objects remaining in it, for any lawful and reputable use, according to the laws of this land.

This building, having now been declared deconsecrated and secularized, I declare to be no longer subject to my canonical jurisdiction.

This Declaration, which is to be publicly proclaimed before witnesses gathered at the said building, is given under my hand and seal, in the *City* of _____, *State* of _____, and Diocese of _____, on this _____ day of _____, in the year of our Lord _____.
    (signed) _____
    Bishop of _____

After the foregoing Declaration has been read, the Presiding Minister says

	The Lord be with you.
People	And also with you.
Minister	Let us pray.

Minister and People

    Our Father . . . .

Then the Presiding Minister says

Lord God, in your great goodness you once accepted to your honor and glory this building, now secularized: Receive our praise and thanksgiving for the blessings, help, and comfort which you bestowed upon your people in this place. Continue, we pray, your many mercies in your Church, that we may be conscious at all times of your unchanging love; through Jesus Christ our Lord. *Amen.*

Assist us mercifully, O Lord, in these our prayers, and dispose the way of your servants towards the attainment of everlasting salvation; that among the swift and varied changes of this world, our hearts may surely there be fixed where true joys are to be found; through Jesus Christ our Lord. *Amen.*

The Lord bless us and keep us. *Amen.*
The Lord make his face to shine upon us,
    and be gracious to us. *Amen.*
The Lord lift up his countenance upon us,
    and give us peace. *Amen.*

The Peace may be exchanged.

Concerning the Rite

The Book of Common Prayer affirms the place of the Holy Eucharist as "the principal act of Christian worship on the Lord's Day and other major Feasts," and thus the foundation of the corporate prayer of the Church. As an act of the whole community of faith, the Eucharist is a summons to all the baptized to share in the table of the Lord. This form for the distribution of Holy Communion by licensed lay persons is intended to foster a corporate sense of the Eucharist among those who, by reason of illness or infirmity, are unable to be present in their church's assembly on Sunday or some other principal feast.

This service is to be conducted by a duly licensed person immediately following such parish celebrations of the Holy Eucharist. The General Convention (1985) has specified that "The Lay Eucharistic Minister shall be limited to the following:

a). Administering the Elements at any Celebration of Holy Eucharist if there is an insufficient number of Priests or Deacons present;

b). Directly following a Celebration of the Holy Eucharist on Sunday or other principle Celebrations, if so authorized by the Member of the Clergy in charge of the Congregation and especially licensed thereto by the Bishop, taking the Sacrament consecrated at the Celebration to those members of the congregation who, by reason of illness or infirmity, were unable to be present at the Celebration."

It is desirable that other parishioners, relatives, and friends also be present to communicate with the person visited. Those so ministered to should also be visited regularly by the clergy of the congregation. In this way, those who are unable to participate regularly in the worship of the eucharistic assembly may nevertheless experience their relation to the community and also join their personal faith and witness to that of their community. It is appropriate that the person be invited to join in commenting on the Scripture and in offering suitable prayers during the rite.

Distribution
of Holy Communion

by Lay Eucharistic Ministers
to persons who are ill or infirm

This form is to be used only immediately after the principal Eucharist on Sunday or other Principal Celebrations.

The Lay Eucharistic Minister should be accompanied by other persons from the congregation.

The Lay Eucharistic Minister greets the people

> The Peace of the Lord be always with you.
>
> *Response*   And also with you.

Collect of the Day

Gospel of the Day, or some other passage of Scripture appropriate to the occasion.

Comments may be made about the sermon of that day.

Suitable prayers may be offered.

A Confession of Sin may be said

> Most merciful God,
> we confess that we have sinned against you

in thought, word, and deed,
by what we have done,
and by what we have left undone.
We have not loved you with our whole heart;
we have not loved our neighbors as ourselves.
We are truly sorry and we humbly repent.
For the sake of your Son Jesus Christ,
have mercy on us and forgive us;
that we may delight in your will,
and walk in your ways,
to the glory of your Name. *Amen.*

Minister May Almighty God in mercy receive our confession
of sorrow and of faith, strengthen us in all
goodness, and by the power of the Holy Spirit keep
us in eternal life. *Amen.*

The Lord's Prayer

Administration of the Holy Communion
(using one of the authorized words of administration)

Closing Prayer

O gracious God, whose Christ stretched out arms of love
upon the hard wood of the cross to embrace all the peoples
of the earth: We give you thanks for feeding *N.* our *sister*
with the Sacrament of that precious Body and Blood, which
is the sign and instrument of our common life, and also for
enriching our parish family by *her* sharing with us the food
of our pilgrimage, the foretaste of that heavenly banquet of
which we shall partake with all your saints; through Jesus
Christ, our Savior. *Amen.*

Minister   Let us bless the Lord.
Response Thanks be to God.

Lay Eucharistic Ministers
specially licensed to take the Sacrament
to those who are ill or infirm.

Suggested Guidelines

1. Lay Eucharistic Ministers must be adult confirmed communicants in good standing, be carefully chosen and trained, and be specially licensed. a candidate is to be recommneded by the cleric in charge of the congregation to the Bishop of the diocese to be licensed. "Such special license shall be given only at the request, and upon the recommendation, of, the Member of the Clergy in charge of the Congregation in which the Lay Eucharistic Minister will be serving. The license shall be issued for a period of time not to exceed three years and shall be revocable at any time by the Bishop, or by the Member of the clergy at whose request it was granted." (Title III, Canon 3, Sec. 2)

2. Where a Deacon serves in a congregation, that minister should supervise the work of the Lay Eucharistic Ministers.

3. It is recommended that the person to be ministered to be prayed for specifically in the Prayers of the People by the congregation on that day.

4. The administration of the Sacrament to the persons visited should take place immediately after the service in the church. Following the communion of the people, the Lay Eucharistic Ministers come forward and are commended for this ministry with the following or similar words:

In the name of this congregation, I send you forth bearing these holy gifts, that those to whom you go may share with us in the communion of Christ's body and blood. We who are many are one body, because we all share one bread, one cup.

5. A suitable container in which to carry the two vessels for the bread and wine, corporals, and purificators is to be supplied. The container is

Distribution of Holy Communion   325

to be returned immediately to the parish along with any unconsumed elements.

6. The people to whom Holy Communion is to be administered are to be notified in advance and the time of the appointment clearly set.

7. Only the order of the rite entitled *"Distribution of Holy Communion by Lay Eucharistic Ministers"* is to be used.

Guidelines for Use on the Occasion of a Retirement or Work Transition

1. The celebration may occur within the context of a Sunday or weekday service. If it occurs during a principal service on Sunday, the proper readings for that Sunday are to be used. Readings for other days may be chosen from Various Occasions 10, 11, 15, 22, 23, 25 (BCP 928-931).

2. Celebrations of a spouse's retirement or career change should uphold the importance of the transition for both partners.

3. The person(s) might be invited by the member of the clergy in charge to serve a special function in the liturgy (such as lector, homilist, eucharistic minister) as appropriate. They should present the bread and wine or receive a special blessing and prayers. Family members or friends might read the Prayers of the People, which could be adapted to the occasion.

4. The rite, whether focused on lay or clerical retirement, has a primary emphasis of baptismal ministry. In constructing the rite, symbols, songs and texts should reflect the person or couple's understanding of their vocation/ministry as the work God has given them to do.

Collect for Work Transitions or Retirement

Gracious God, we thank you for the work and witness of your servant(s) N. (and N.) who *has (have)* enriched this community and brought gladness to friends (and family); now bless and preserve *him* at this time of transition. Guide *him* in the continued use of your gifts. Give *him* sustenance for temporal and spiritual needs, friends to cheer *his* way, and a clear vision of the ministry to which you are now calling *him*. By your Holy Spirit be present in *his* pilgrimage, that *he* may travel with the One who is the Way, the Truth, and the Life, Jesus Christ our Lord. *Amen.*

Episcopal Services

Consecration of Chrism Apart from Baptism

Provision is made in the rite of Holy Baptism for the consecration of Chrism in local congregations for use by a priest at baptisms in that church which take place on subsequent occasions in the year.

The following form is intended for use when, because of the absence of candidates for Baptism, the consecration of Chrism takes place at the time of Confirmation (see the last rubric on page 419 of the Prayer Book), or at some other time. The rite takes place immediately after the postcommunion prayer, and before the bishop's blessing and the dismissal.

The olive oil to be consecrated should be prepared in an ampulla or other vessel large enough to be seen clearly by the congregation. Traditionally, a small amount of oil of balsam or other fragrant oil is added to it, either before the service, or just before the consecratory prayer.

If desired, the vessel of oil may be brought forward in the offertory procession, received by a deacon or other minister, and then placed on a convenient side table until needed.

Immediately after the postcommunion prayer, the ampulla is brought to the bishop, who places it on a small table in the sight of the congregation, or on the altar (the communion vessels having already been removed).

Dear Friends in Christ: In the beginning, the Spirit of God hovered over the creation; and, throughout history, God, by the gift of the Holy Spirit, has empowered his people to serve him. As a sign of that gift, the priests and kings of Israel were anointed with oil; and our Lord Jesus was himself anointed with the Holy Spirit at his Baptism as the Christ, God's own Messiah. At Baptism, Christians are likewise anointed by that same Spirit to empower them for God's service. Let us now set apart this oil to be the sign of that anointing.

Let us pray. *(Silence)*

The Bishop then places a hand on the vessel of oil and prays

Eternal Father, whose blessed Son was anointed by the Holy Spirit to be the Savior and servant of all, we pray you to consecrate this oil, that those who are sealed with it may share in the royal priesthood of Jesus Christ; who lives and reigns with you and the Holy Spirit, for ever and ever. *Amen.*

The Liturgy then concludes in the usual way with the Bishop's blessing and the dismissal.

A Proper for the Consecration of Chrism

If there is a need to consecrate Chrism at a separate, diocesan, service the following Proper may be used:

Collect

Almighty God, who by the power of the Holy Spirit anointed your Son to be Messiah and Priest for ever, grant that all whom you have called to his service may confess the faith of Christ crucified, proclaim his resurrection, and share in his eternal priesthood; who lives and reigns with you in the unity of the same Spirit, one God, now and for ever. *Amen.*

Old Testament   Isaiah 61:1 -8
Psalm   23,   *or*   89:20-29
Epistle   Revelation 1:4-8
Gospel   Luke 4:16-21

The Chrism is consecrated as described on page 234.

Reaffirmation of Ordination Vows

This form is intended for use at a celebration of the Eucharist upon an occasion when the clergy are gathered together with the bishop.

It may also be used on the occasion of the reception of a priest from another Communion or of a restoration to the ministry.

If the Renewal of Ordination Vows takes place on Maundy Thursday, it should be done at a celebration of the Eucharist other than the Proper Liturgy of the day.

The following Collect may be used

Almighty God, giver of all good gifts, in your divine providence you have appointed various orders of ministers in your Church: Give your grace, we humbly pray, to all who are called to any office and ministry for your people; and so fill them with the truth of your doctrine, and clothe them with holiness of life, that they may faithfully serve before you, to the glory of your great Name and for the benefit of your holy Church; through Jesus Christ our Lord, who lives and reigns with you, in the unity of the Holy Spirit, one God, now and for ever. *Amen.*

The Psalm and Lessons may be those appointed for Ordination, or those for the Celebration of a New Ministry.

After the Sermon (and Creed), the Bishop sits in a chair before the Altar and addresses those who are to renew their vows. They stand facing the Bishop, who says these or similar words

Dear friends, the ministry we share is none other than the sacrificial ministry of Christ, who gave himself up to death on the cross for the salvation of the world. By his glorious resurrection he has opened for us the way of everlasting life. By the gift of the Holy Spirit he shares with us the riches of his grace.

We are called to proclaim his death and resurrection, to administer the Sacraments of the New Covenant which he sealed with his blood on the cross, and to care for his people in the power of the Spirit.

Do you here, in the presence of Christ and his Church, renew your commitment to your ministry, under the pastoral direction of your bishop?

Answer	I do.
Bishop	Do you reaffirm your promise to give yourself to prayer and study?
Answer	I do.
Bishop	Do you reaffirm your promise so to minister the Word of God and the Sacraments of the New Covenant that the reconciling love of Christ may be known and received?
Answer	I do.
Bishop	Do you reaffirm your promise to be a faithful servant of all those committed to your care, patterning your life in accordance with the teachings of Christ, so that you may be a wholesome example to your people?
Answer	I do.

The Bishop then stands and makes this affirmation

And now, as your bishop, I, too, before God and you, re-dedicate myself and reaffirm the promises that I made when I was ordained. I ask your prayers.

Bishop and Clergy

May the Lord who has given us the will to do these things, give us also the grace and power to perform them.

The Bishop then says

The peace of the Lord be always with you.
People   And also with you.

The Peace is then exchanged throughout the congregation.

The service continues with the Prayers of the People, or with the Offertory.

When this form is used for the reception of a priest from another Communion as a priest in this Church (the canonical requirements having been fulfilled), or for a restoration to the ministry, the service may be adapted as necessary, and the following question and answer are inserted immediately before the bishop's affirmation at the top of this page.

Will you be loyal to the doctrine, discipline, and worship of Christ as this Church has received them? And will you, in accordance with the canons of this Church, obey your bishop and other ministers who may have authority over you and your work?

Answer

I am willing and ready to do so; and I solemnly declare that I do believe the Holy Scriptures of the Old and New Testament to be the Word of God, and to contain all things necessary to salvation; and I do solemnly engage to conform to the doctrine, discipline, and worship of The Episcopal Church.

The newly received or restored priest is greeted personally by the bishop at the exchange of the Peace, and, having put on the vestments proper to the order, stands at the Altar with the bishop as a concelebrant at the Eucharist.

A newly restored deacon is greeted in the same way, and, properly vested, prepares the bread and wine at the Offertory.

Concerning the Service

This order is provided for use when a priest in charge of a congregation terminates a pastoral relationship. In other circumstances, appropriate actions of this rite may be used, and necessary alterations may be made.

It is the prerogative of the bishop to be present and to act as chief minister, or to appoint a deputy. However, the congregation and the departing minister may take leave of each other without the presence of the bishop or the bishop's representative. It is suggested that this service take place within a Eucharist, which begins in the usual way.

A Service for the Ending of a Pastoral Relationship and Leave-taking from a Congregation

At the Service of the Word

A hymn, psalm, or anthem may be sung.

The people standing, the Celebrant says,

	Blessed be God: Father, Son, and Holy Spirit.
People	And blessed be his kingdom, now and forever. *Amen.*

In place of the above, for Easter Day through the Day of Pentecost

Celebrant	Alleluia. Christ is risen.
People	The Lord is risen indeed. Alleluia.

In Lent and on other penitential occasions

Celebrant	Bless the Lord who forgives all our sins;
People	His mercy endures for ever.

The Celebrant then continues

	There is one Body and one Spirit;
People	There is one hope in God's call to us;
Celebrant	One Lord, one Faith, one Baptism;
People	One God and Father of all.

Celebrant	The Lord be with you.
People	And also with you.
Celebrant	Let us pray.

The Collect of the Day

At the principal service on a Sunday or other feast, the collect and lessons are properly those of the day. At other times, one of the following collects may be used.

Almighty and everlasting God, by whose Spirit the whole body of your faithful people is governed and sanctified: Receive our supplications and prayers, which we offer before you for all members of your holy Church, that in their vocation and ministry they may truly and devoutly serve you; through our Lord and Savior Jesus Christ, who lives and reigns with you and the Holy Spirit, one God, now and for ever. *Amen.*

O God of unchangeable power and eternal light: Look favorably on your whole Church, that wonderful and sacred mystery; by the effectual working of your providence, carry out in tranquility the plan of salvation; let the whole world see and know that things which were cast down are being raised up, and things which had grown old are being made new, and that all things are being brought to their perfection by him through whom all things were made, your Son Jesus Christ our Lord; who lives and reigns with you, in the unity of the Holy Spirit, one God, for ever and ever. *Amen.*

Direct us, O Lord, in all our doings with *thy* most gracious favor, and further us with *thy* continual help; that in all our works begun, continued, and ended in *thee,* we may glorify *thy* holy Name, and finally, by *thy* mercy, obtain everlasting life; through Jesus Christ our Lord. *Amen.*

Gracious Father, we pray for thy holy Catholic Church. Fill it with all truth, in all truth with all peace. Where it is corrupt, purify it; where it is in error, direct it; where in any thing it is amiss, reform it. Where it is right, strengthen it; where it is in want, provide for it; where it is divided, reunite it; for the sake of Jesus Christ thy Son our Savior. *Amen.*

Almighty Father, whose blessed Son before his passion prayed for his disciples that they might be one, as you and he are one: Grant that your Church, being bound together in love and obedience to you, may be united in one body by the one Spirit, that the world may believe in him whom you have sent, your Son Jesus Christ our Lord; who lives and reigns with you, in the unity of the Holy Spirit, one God, now and for ever. *Amen.*

or this collect

Lord, you have apportioned to your people the manifold gifts of the Spirit: Grant amid the changes of the world that your Church may abide, and be strengthened in ministry through continuous outpouring of your gifts; through Jesus Christ our Lord, who lives and reigns with you and the Holy Spirit, one God, for ever and ever. *Amen.*

The Ministry of the Word

Old Testament

Genesis 31:44-46,48-49,50b (The Lord watch between you and me when we are absent one from another.)

Genesis 12:1-9 (Abraham's departure from Haran and God's promise to bless him.)

Deuteronomy 18:15-18 (God will raise up a prophet like Moses.)

Deuteronomy 32:1-9 (The farewell of Moses.)

Joshua 24:1,14-25 (Joshua's farewell to his people.)

Ecclesiastes 3:1-7;7:8,10,13-14 (A time for everything; better the end than the beginning.)

Sirach 50:1,11-24 (The service of the faithful priest.)

Psalm 119:89-96, *or* Nunc Dimittis

Epistle

1 Corinthians 3:4-11 (Paul planted, Apollos watered, God gave growth.)
Acts 16:9-10 (Paul's call from Macedonia.)
Acts 20:17-22,25-28,32,36-38b (Paul's apologia for his ministry at
   Ephesus.)
II Thessalonians 2:13—3:5 (Paul gives thanks for the success of the
   Gospel.)
I Thessalonians 5:12-25 (Paul encourages the ministry among the
   Thessalonians.)
Philippians 4:1-10,23 (Rejoice in the Lord always.)

Alleluia Verse: Alleluia. "I will instruct you in the way that you should
go; I will guide you with my eye says the Lord." Alleluia. (Psalm 32:9 or
Psalm 25:9) Tract; Psalm 18:33-37; Psalm 43:3-6; Psalm 78:1-8; Psalm
133.

Gospel

Matthew 9:35-38 (The harvest is plentiful, but the laborers are few.)
Matthew 25:31-40 (As you did it to the least of these, you did it to me.)
Luke 12:35-38 (The faithful servant.)
Luke 17:7-10 (We are unworthy servants; we have only done our duty.)
John 10:14-18 (The ministry of the good shepherd.)
John 21:15-19 (Feed my sheep.)

Sermon

*It maybe appropriate for the Bishop or the Bishop's Deputy to preach the
sermon, in the course of which a charge should be given to the
congregation regarding the nature of ministry.*

The service continues with the Nicene Creed.

The Ending of a Pastoral Relationship

Just before the Peace, the Minister addresses the Bishop (or the Bishop's Deputy) and the congregation with these or similar words

On the _____ day of _____, 19___, I was inducted by Bishop N. as rector of _____. I have, with God's help and to the best of my abilities, exercised this trust, accepting its priveleges and responsibilities.

After prayer and careful consideration, it now seems to me that I should leave this charge, and I publicly state that my tenure as rector of _____ ends this day.

(The Minister may, if desired, briefly state his plans for the future.)

The Bishop or the Deputy says

Do you, the people of _____, recognize and accept the conclusion of this pastoral relationship?

People   We do.

If the Bishop or Bishop's Deputy is not present, the Minister may address a similar question to the congregation.

Then the Minister may express thanksgiving for the time of the tenure, with its joys and sorrows, and state hopes for the future of the congregation.

The Minister may present to the warden(s) a letter of resignation, the keys of the parish, the parish altar service book, the parish register, or other symbols fitting to the occasion.

The Minister may also express his thanks to the representatives of parish organizations and offices, and indicate that those organizations will continue to function.

The Minister may then be joined by members of his family, who may express what life with the congregation has meant to them. One or more representatives of the congregation may briefly respond to the Minister and family, and bid them godspeed. If it is appropriate, representatives of diocesan and community organizations in which the Minister or members of his family have been active may also speak.

The Bishop or the Bishop's Deputy may then indicate what provision has been made for the continuation of the ministries of the parish. He may declare the name of the locum tenens, senior warden, or other person who is to have ecclesiastical responsibility, and may request, if it seems appropriate, other leaders in the parish to continue their leadership until a new incumbent is installed. He may express his feelings about the ministry now coming to its end.

The departing Minister and the congregation then say together the following prayer

O God, you have bound us together for a time as priest and people to work for the advancement of your kingdom in this place: We give you humble and hearty thanks for the ministry which we have shared in these years now past.

Silence

We thank you for your patience with us despite our blindness and slowness of heart. We thank you for your forgiveness and mercy in the face of our many failures.

Silence

Especially we thank you for your never-failing presence with us through these years, and for the deeper knowledge of you and of each other which we have attained.

Silence

We thank you for those who have been joined to this part of Christ's family through baptism. We thank you for opening our hearts and minds again and again to your Word, and for feeding us abundantly with the Sacrament of the Body and Blood of your Son.

Silence

Now, we pray, be with those who leave and with us who stay; and grant that all of us, by drawing ever nearer to you, may always be close to each other in the communion of your saints. All this we ask for the sake of Jesus Christ, your Son, our Lord. *Amen.*

The departing Minister, or the Bishop, or the Bishop's Deputy then says

The peace of the Lord be always with you
People   And also with you.

If the Eucharist is to follow, the service continues with the offertory.

Except on major feasts, the Preface may be that for Apostles and Ordinations.

After the Communion

Almighty God, we thank you for feeding us with the holy food of the Body and Blood of your Son, and for uniting us through him in the fellowship of your Holy Spirit. We thank you for raising up among us faithful servants of your Word and Sacraments. We thank you especially for the work of N. among us, *and the presence of* his *family here.* Grant that both *he* and we may serve you in the days ahead, and always rejoice in your glory, and come at length into your heavenly kingdom; through Jesus Christ our Lord. *Amen.*

This blessing may be pronounced either by the minister, or by the bishop, or by the Bishop's Deputy.

May God, who has led us in the paths of justice and truth, lead us still, and keep us in his ways. *Amen.*

May God, whose Son has loved us and given himself for us, love us still, and establish us in peace. *Amen.*

May God, whose Spirit unites us and fills our hearts with joy, illumine us still, and strengthen us for the years to come. *Amen.*

And the blessing of God Almighty, the Father, the Son, and the Holy Spirit, be upon you and remain with you for ever. *Amen.*

If the departing Minister is the Celebrant, one of the post-communion prayers from the Book of Common Prayer, Holy Eucharist, Rite Two, pages 365-366, will be more appropriate.

Concerning the Service

This rite is designed for the recognition, investiture (and seating) of a bishop who has previously been ordained and consecrated in and for another diocese. It may be adapted to the circumstances of a former suffragan bishop who has been elected as diocesan bishop, or for a former bishop coadjutor who succeeds to the see.

The Presiding Bishop of the Church, or another bishop deputized for the occasion, presides at the rite.

The President of the Standing Committee of the Diocese serves as Warden.

Representative presbyters, deacons, and lay persons are assigned appropriate duties in the service.

The Readings and Psalm may be selected from the Proper of the Day, from those appointed for the Ordination of a Bishop, or from those appointed for Various Occasions.

The rubrics envisage the service taking place in the Cathedral Church. It may, however, be held in some other suitable place, and the service may be adapted when necessary.

One adaptation which will frequently need to be made is the omission of the seating of the bishop in the cathedra. In this case, immediately following the taking of the oath, the Presiding Bishop invites the people to greet their new bishop. The people offer their acclamations and applause, and the service continues with the exchange of the peace.

If a pastoral staff is used, it is carried by the former bishop in the welcoming procession, and presented to the new bishop at the time appointed. In the absence of the former bishop, it is placed on the Altar before the service begins.

The Bible to be used at the taking of the Oath is placed on the Altar before the beginning of the service.

If, for any reason, there is no Communion, the service concludes after the Peace with the singing of a hymn or anthem, the Lord's Prayer, the bishop's blessing, and the dismissal.

Recognition and Investiture
of a Diocesan Bishop

The Recognition

*When the ministers and people have assembled in the Cathedral Church,
the principal doors having been closed, the Presiding Bishop is escorted
from the sacristy to a chair placed at the entrance to the chancel, facing
the people.*

*A welcoming procession is formed, and moves through the congregation
to the principal door.*

*The new Bishop, attended by two deacons, standing outside the door,
knocks upon it three times.*

*The Warden opens the door. As the door is opened, the Bishop's voice is
heard, saying*

Open for me the gates of righteousness; I will enter them and
give thanks to the Lord.

Warden   The Lord prosper you;
               we wish you well in the Name of the Lord.

*A psalm or anthem is sung, during which the bishop is escorted by the
welcoming procession to a place before the Presiding Bishop. Psalm 23
is appropriate, with the following antiphon*

I will give you a shepherd after my own heart, who will feed you with knowledge and understanding.

The new Bishop petitions as follows

I, N.N., whom God has ordained to be a shepherd and servant, and who now have been chosen as Bishop of this Diocese, come to you, desiring to be recognized, and invested, [and seated in the chair which is the symbol of that office].

The Presiding Bishop replies

Before I can accede to your petition, we must be assured by the appointed representative of the Diocese that you will be received as their duly elected Bishop.

The Warden then says

We are ready and willing to do so. As President of the Standing Committee, I certify that N.N. was duly elected Bishop of the Diocese of _____ by the clergy and people in Diocesan Convention assembled on the _____ day of_____, _____, and that consents to the election have been received from (a majority of the Bishops of the Church having jurisdiction and of the Standing Committees of the Dioceses) (the two houses of the General Convention). We therefore present to you the Right Reverend N.N. to be invested for the exercise of the office to which *he* has been chosen.

The Presiding Bishop then says

Let the will of the people here present be made known. Do you recognize and receive N. as your Bishop?

People　　　We do.

Presiding Bishop

Will you uphold N. in this ministry?

People   We will.

The Presiding Bishop stands and calls the people to prayer, in these or similar words

Let us now offer our prayers for N., for this Diocese, and for all God's people.

All kneel, and the Person appointed leads the Litany for Ordinations, or some other approved litany. At the end of the litany, after the Kyries (which may be sung by the congregation or choir in threefold, sixfold, or ninefold form), the Presiding Bishop stands and says

          The Lord be with you.

People   And also with you.

Presiding Bishop   Let us pray.

The Presiding Bishop then says the Collect of the Day or the Collect for Ordination.

All sit, and the Liturgy of the Word continues in the usual manner.

After the Sermon (and Creed), the following renewal of the commitments of ordination may take place.

The Presiding Bishop addresses the new Bishop in these or similar words

My *brother,* it has pleased God to call you to be the shepherd and chief pastor of this Diocese. I am sure that long before now you have laid to heart the high trust and weighty obligations of this office. But, in order that this congregation may know your commitment to fulfill this trust, I call upon you to reaffirm the promises you made when you were ordained and consecrated a bishop.

	Will you exercise your ministry in obedience to Christ?
Answer	I will obey Christ, and will serve in his name.
Presiding Bishop	Will you be faithful in prayer, and in the study of Holy Scripture, that you may have the mind of Christ?
Answer	I will, for he is my help.
Presiding Bishop	Will you boldly proclaim and interpret the Gospel of Christ, enlightening the minds and stirring up the conscience of your people?
Answer	I will, in the power of the Spirit.
Presiding Bishop	As chief priest and pastor, will you encourage and support all baptized people in their gifts and ministries, nourish them from the riches of God's grace, pray for them without ceasing, and celebrate with them the sacraments of our redemption?
Answer	I will, in the name of Christ, the Shepherd and Bishop of our souls.
Presiding Bishop	Will you guard the faith, unity, and discipline of the Church?
Answer	I will, for the love of God.
Presiding Bishop	Will you share with your fellow bishops in the government of the whole Church; will you sustain your fellow presbyters and take counsel with them; will you guide and strengthen the deacons and all others who minister in the Church?
Answer	I will, by the grace given me.
Presiding Bishop	Will you be merciful to all, show compassion to the poor and strangers, and defend those who have no helper?
Answer	I will, for the sake of Jesus Christ.

Presiding Bishop	May the Lord who has given you the will to do these things, give you the grace and power to perform them.
Answer	Amen.

The Investiture

The Presiding Bishop now stands and says

My *brother*, you have been recognized as a bishop of the Church and as bishop of this Diocese. Now I, N.N., by the authority committed to me, and with the consent of those who have chosen you, do invest you, N.N., as Bishop of _____, with all the temporal and spiritual rights and responsibilities that pertain to that office; in the Name of the Father, and of the Son, and of the Holy Spirit. *Amen.*

If a pastoral staff is to be given, it is presented by the former Bishop of the Diocese, or it is brought from the Altar and presented by the Warden. The one who delivers the staff says

On behalf of the people and clergy of the Diocese of _____, I give into your hands this pastoral staff. May Christ the good Shepherd uphold you and sustain you as you carry it in his name. *Amen.*

A Bible is brought from the Altar and held before the Bishop, who, laying a hand upon it, takes the oath, as follows

I, N.N., Bishop in the Church of God, now duly invested and acknowledged as Bishop of this Diocese [receive this pastoral staff at your hands as a token of my jurisdiction and of your recognition, and] do solemnly promise that I will observe, and to the utmost of my power fulfill, the responsibilities and obligations of this office, striving in all things to be a faithful shepherd to the flock of Christ. So help me God. *Amen.*

The Seating

The Presiding Bishop and the Warden now escort the bishop to the chair designated for the Bishop of the Diocese. Meanwhile, instrumental music may be played.

The Dean of the Cathedral Church, meeting the Bishop at the Cathedra, says

In the name of *the Chapter* of this Cathedral Church, and on behalf of the people of this Diocese, I install you, N., in the chair appointed to your office. May the Lord stir up in you the flame of holy charity, and the power of faith that overcomes the world. *Amen.*

The Bishop sits, and the People offer their acclamations and applause.

Bells may be rung and trumpets sounded.

Afterwards, the Bishop stands and says

The peace of the Lord be always with you.

People   And also with you.

The Presiding Bishop and other Ministers greet the Bishop.

The People greet one another.

The Bishop greets other members of the clergy, family members, and members of the congregation as may be convenient.

The Liturgy continues with the Offertory.

Deacons prepare the Table.

The Bishop goes to the Lord's Table as chief Celebrant and, joined by other bishops and representative presbyters of the diocese, proceeds with the celebration of the Eucharist.

In place of the usual postcommunion prayer, a Bishop or Presbyter leads the people in the following

Almighty Father, we thank you for feeding us with the holy food of the Body and Blood of your Son, and for uniting us through him in the fellowship of your Holy Spirit. We thank you for raising up among us faithful servants for the ministry of your Word and Sacraments. We pray that N. may be to us an effective example in word and action, in love and patience, and in holiness of life. Grant that we, with *him,* may serve you now, and always rejoice in your glory; through Jesus Christ your Son our Lord, who lives and reigns with you and the Holy Spirit, one God, now and for ever. *Amen.*

The new Bishop blesses the people, first saying

	Our help is in the name of the Lord;
People	The maker of heaven and earth.
Bishop	Blessed be the name of the Lord;
People	From this time forth for evermore.
Bishop	The blessing, mercy, and grace of God Almighty, the Father, the Son, and the Holy Spirit, be upon you, and remain with you for ever. *Amen.*

A Deacon dismisses the People.

Concerning the Service

This service is intended for use when a new bishop has not been seated in the cathedra of the diocese at the time of ordination or at the time of recognition and investiture.

Normally, it will take place on the occasion of the first visit of the bishop to the Cathedral.

On a Sunday or other major Holy Day the Proper is that of the Day. On other days it may be one of those appointed for Various Occasions.

If, however, the seating takes place shortly after the service of ordination or investure held on the same day in a place other than the Cathedral, only the opening ceremonies of this service are used, concluding after the Te Deum or Gloria in excelsis with the Lord's Prayer, the bishop's blessing, and the dismissal.

Welcoming and Seating
of a Bishop in the Cathedral

The ministers and people assemble in the Cathedral Church.

*The principal door being closed, the Dean, the Cathedral clergy (the
Cathedral Chapter), and other representative persons as convenient, go
in procession through the congregation to the principal door. The people
stand.*

*The new bishop, attended by two deacons, standing outside, knocks
three times on the door.*

*The Warden opens the door, and the Bishop enters and greets the
congregation, saying*

Grace and peace be with you, from God our Father and the
Lord Jesus Christ.

People　　　And also with you.

*A psalm or anthem is sung, during which the Bishop is escorted by the
welcoming procession to a place in full sight of the people.*

*The Dean, or other person appointed, welcomes the bishop in these or
similar words*

N.N., Bishop in the Church of God, and our Bishop, we
welcome you to your Cathedral Church, the symbol and
center of your pastoral, liturgical, and teaching ministry in
this Diocese.

The Bishop responds, saying

I, *N.N.*, your Bishop, thank you for your welcome. I promise, God helping me, to be a faithful shepherd and servant among you. I pray that the ministry which we will share may be pleasing to God, and that it may strengthen the life of this diocese, and the whole Church of God. I now ask to be seated in the chair that is the symbol of my office.

The bishop is escorted to the Cathedra. Meanwhile, instrumental music may be played.

The Dean, standing near the Cathedra, says

In the name of *the Chapter* of this Cathedral Church, and on behalf of the people of this diocese, I install you, *N.*, in the chair appointed to your office. May the Lord stir up in you the flame of holy charity, and the power of faith that overcomes the world. *Amen.*

The Bishop sits, and the People offer their acclamations and applause.

Bells may be rung and trumpets sounded.

The Bishop stands, and the Te Deum, the Gloria in excelsis, or other song of praise is sung.

The Bishop then says to the people

	The Lord be with you.
People	And also with you.
Bishop	Let us pray.

The Bishop says the Collect of the Day.

The Liturgy continues in the usual way, with the appointed Lessons and Psalm.

At the Great Thanksgiving, the Bishop, as the principal Celebrant, is joined at the Altar by the presbyters of the Cathedral, and other priests as desired.

In place of the usual postcommunion prayer, the Dean leads the people in the following

Almighty Father, we thank you for feeding us with the holy food of the Body and Blood of your Son, and for uniting us through him in the fellowship of your Holy Spirit. We thank you for raising up among us faithful servants for the ministry of your Word and Sacraments. We pray that N. may be to us an effective example in word and action, in love and patience, and in holiness of life. Grant that we, with *him* may serve you now, and always rejoice in your glory; through Jesus Christ your Son our Lord, who lives and reigns with you and the Holy Spirit, one God, now and for ever. *Amen.*

The Bishop blesses the people, first saying

| | Our help is in the Name of the Lord. |
| *People* | The maker of heaven and earth. |

| *Bishop* | Blessed be the Name of the Lord. |
| *People* | From this time forth for evermore. |

| *Bishop* | The blessing, mercy, and grace of God Almighty, the Father, the Son, and the Holy Spirit, be upon you and remain with you for ever. *Amen.* |

A Deacon dismisses the people.

Setting Apart
for a Special Vocation

Individual Christians, in response to God's call, may wish to commit themselves to the religious life under vows made directly to the bishop of the diocese.

The order which follows is not intended to supplant forms in use for admitting members to religious communities.

Where life profession is intended, the process normally involves three stages: novitiate, temporary or annual vows, and life profession. In some instances, persons may choose not to proceed beyond the stage of annual vows.

The novitiate is a period of testing. Admission to the novitiate normally takes place at a weekday Daily Office, at the time of the hymn or anthem which follows the Collects. It involves a promise to accept and follow a specific and agreed-upon rule of life for a period of time prescribed by the bishop.

Temporary or annual vows are made at the satisfactory conclusion of the prescribed period of testing. At this time, the person takes vows of poverty, chastity, and obedience to the bishop, for a prescribed length of time. This stage involves the acceptance of the obligation to recite an approved form of the Daily Office. The rite takes place at a celebration of the Holy Eucharist, immediately after the Prayers of the People and before the Peace. Appropriate clothing may be presented as a sign of dedication.

Final or life vows are made at a festal celebration of the Holy Eucharist. At this time additional symbols of dedication may be given.

The order of the rite is identical for all three stages.

1. A request by the person to be admitted to the appropriate stage.

2. A sermon or homily, or an address to the person.

3. An examination by the bishop concerning the nature of the commitment and of the person's desire for this special vocation.

4. The promises or vows appropriate to the stage of profession.

5. The appropriate prayer or blessing appended to this order, or some other similar form.

6. The presentation of clothing and other symbols of special vocation.

Appropriate Lessons and Psalms

Old Testament

Genesis 12:1-4a(4b-8) (The Call of Abraham)
1 Samuel 3:1-11 (The Call of Samuel)
1 Kings 19:16b,19-21 (The Call of Elisha)

Psalms

23 (The Lord is my shepherd)
24:1-6(7-10) (Who can ascend the hill of the Lord?)
27:1-11(12-18) (Your face, Lord, will I seek)
33:(1-11)12-22 (The eye of the Lord is upon those who fear him)
34:1-8(9-22) (I will bless the Lord at all times)
40:1-12 (I love to do your will, O my God)
63:1-12 (You are my God; eagerly I seek you)
100 (Serve the Lord with gladness)

New Testament

Acts 2:42-47 (The apostles' teaching and fellowship)
Acts 4:32-35 (They had everything in common)

1 Corinthians 1:22-31 (God chose what was foolish)
Philippians 3:8-14 (That I may gain Christ)
Colossians 3:12-17 (Put on love, which binds everything together)
1 John 4:7-16 (He who abides in love abides in God)

The Gospel

Matthew 16:24-27 (Let him take up his cross and follow me)
Matthew 19:3-12 (Eunuchs for the sake of the kingdom)
Matthew 19:16-26 (Sell what you possess and give to the poor)
John 15:1-8 (I am the vine, you are the branches)

Prayer for a Novice

Look with favor, Almighty God, upon this your servant N.,
who, in response to the prompting of the Holy Spirit, desires
to commit *himself* to you in a life of special vocation, and is
undertaking to embrace the three-fold path of poverty,
chastity, and obedience. Grant *him* the strength of your
grace to persevere in *his* endeavor, and the guidance of the
Spirit to find *his* true vocation. If it be your will that *he*
continue in this way, reveal this to *him,* we pray, and bring
him in due time to the taking of solemn vows; through Jesus
Christ our Lord, who lives and reigns with you and the Holy
Spirit, one God, for ever and ever. *Amen.*

Dedication of a Person Taking Temporary or Annual Vows

May God the Lord, who called Abraham to leave home and
kindred to journey to an unknown destination, and who led
the people of Israel by the hand of Moses his servant
through the desert to the promised land: Shepherd you in
your pilgrimage, and lead you by safe pathways, for his
Name's sake. *Amen.*

May God the Son, who, in his earthly life, was often solitary but never alone, because the Father was with him: Be your constant companion in your withdrawals from the busyness of the world, and support and strengthen you when you return refreshed to bear witness to the love and power of God. *Amen.*

May God the Holy Spirit, who helps us in our weakness, and intercedes for the saints in accordance with the Father's will: Teach you to pray as you ought to pray; strengthen you in purity of faith, in holiness of life, and in perfectness of love; and bind you ever more and more closely to the Father through the Son. *Amen.*

And may Almighty God, the holy and undivided Trinity, Father, Son, and Holy Spirit, guard your body, save your soul, and bring you safely to the heavenly country; where he lives and reigns for ever and ever. *Amen.*

Dedication of a Person Taking Life Vows

Blessed are you, O Lord our God, for your great love in sending into the world your only-begotten Son, who for us and for our salvation, emptied himself of his divine estate, and embraced a life apart from the consolations of family, having not even a place to lay his head. We bless your Name, also, that in every age and land you have called men and women to imitate their Lord, by setting zeal for your kingdom and its righteousness ahead of all worldly considerations, the love of your little ones above the claims of flesh and blood, and obedience to your will in place of all personal ambitions.

Accept, we pray, the life profession of this your servant *N.* who, following the example of the Lord Jesus, of Anna the prophetess and holy Simeon, of the Lady Julian and Nicholas Ferrar [of _____], and of countless others of your saints, now offers *himself* for your service in a life of poverty, chastity, and obedience. Bestow upon *him* your Holy Spirit to dwell in *him* richly, to give *him* steadfastness of purpose, to sanctify *him* more and more fully, and to guide *him* surely into paths of service and of witness, to the honor and glory of your great Name; through Jesus Christ our Lord, who with you and the Holy Spirit lives and reigns, one God, now and for ever. *Amen.*